A Guide to the Criminal Appeal Act 1995

A Guide to the Criminal Appeal Act 1995

Leonard Jason-Lloyd

Lecturer in Law, University of Derby, and visiting Lecturer in Law at the Midlands Centre for Criminology and Criminal Justice, Loughborough University and the Scarman Centre for the Study of Public Order at the University of Leicester

FRANK CASS

LONDON • PORTLAND, OR.

Published in 1997 in Great Britain by
FRANK CASS & CO. LTD.
Newbury House, 900 Eastern Avenue
London IG2 7HH

and in the United States of America by
FRANK CASS
c/o ISBS, 5804 N.E. Hassalo Street
Portland, Oregon 97213-3644

British Library Cataloguing in Publication Data

Jason-Lloyd, Leonard
A guide to the Criminal Appeal Act 1995
1. Great Britain. Criminal Appeal Act 1995 2. Criminal procedure – England 3. Appellate procedure – England
I. Title
344.2′078
ISBN 0-7146-4791-8 (cloth)
ISBN 0-7146-4285-1 (paper)

Library of Congress Cataloging-in-Publication Data

A catalog record of this book is available from the Library of Congress.

Typeset by Vitaset, Paddock Wood, Kent
Printed in Great Britain by
Bookcraft (Bath) Ltd, Midsomer Norton, Avon

Contents

Acknowledgements

The Criminal Appeal Act 1995 is under Crown copyright and has been reproduced with the permission of the Controller of Her Majesty's Stationery Office.

Preface

The spate of miscarriages of justice that, in large part, prompted the setting up of the Royal Commission on Criminal Justice (which reported in July 1993, Cm 2263) inevitably called into question the system's ability not merely to prevent such warts on the face of criminal justice but also to put in place, in the appellate and extra-curial procedures, the means of redressing the injustices of jury verdicts. Hence the emergence of the Criminal Appeal Act 1995. Mr Jason-Lloyd provides a useful service to busy practitioners engaged in the criminal appeal process with a ready-reckoner as to what the changes in the new regime are. It is a guide, not a commentary or critique. One hopes, however, that his efforts will not stop here. He is well equipped to give further assistance to those who administer the criminal appeal system.

Two, quite disparate issues strike me as significant. First, there is the legislature's determination to put an end to the ceaselessly disputed criteria for allowing an appeal against conviction. The second matter relates to the constitutional displacement of the power of the Home Secretary to refer cases back to the Court of Appeal, in favour of an independent review body.

In the first draft of the Criminal Appeal Bill of 1907 the Court of Criminal Appeal was to be empowered to quash a conviction on any ground upon which the verdict of a jury might be set aside in a civil case – in other words, that the verdict was such as no jury on the evidence (and properly instructed by the trial judge) could reasonably return: a kind of criminal *Wednesbury* rule. During the Bill's parliamentary passage, Mr F.E. Smith (later Lord Birkenhead, Lord Chancellor) urged that the power was much too limited. He moved an amendment which would have required the court to quash a conviction where the verdict of guilty was, in the opinion of the court, 'under all the circumstances of the case unsafe or unsatisfactory'. The Attorney-General of the day, Sir John Walton, expressed sympathy with the spirit of the amendment, but thought that the words were too loose and obscure. Section 4(1) of the 1907

Act was ultimately agreed to without debate. It provided that an appeal shall be allowed if the court thought that the verdict of the jury 'should be set aside on the ground that it is unreasonable or cannot be supported having regard to the evidence, ... or of a wrong decision of any question of law or that on any ground there was a miscarriage of justice'.

That formula stood for 60 years, although on occasion the Court of Criminal Appeal acted as though the test of 'unsafe or unsatisfactory' was the proper one. The Report of the Interdepartmental Committee on the Court of Criminal Appeal in 1965 (the Donovan Committee, Cmnd. 2755) recommended adoption of F.E. Smith's proposal that the new Court of Appeal (Criminal Division) should be given an express power to allow an appeal where, upon consideration of the whole of the evidence, it comes to the conclusion that the verdict is unsafe or unsatisfactory. Parliament agreed. Under the Criminal Appeal Act 1968 that formula was accepted. It has proved, over the last 30 years, to be no less unsatisfactory among the judiciary. As Mr Jason-Lloyd explains, during the second reference of the Birmingham Six to the Court of Appeal, the Court took the view that the words did not have different meanings, but provided alternative terminology. Section 2(1) of the Criminal Appeal Act 1995 now obligingly removes the superfluity of two words to convey a single meaning. Parliament has opted for 'unsafe' simpliciter. Was it right to go for the single, simple Anglo-Saxon word 'safe', instead of the Latinism of 'satisfactory'? It may be logical to say that a conviction, the safety of which is in doubt, is like an unsafe ladder – one whose condition must be regarded as unsatisfactory. But the ladder is unsafe if its physical condition is demonstrably defective. The safety of the conviction relates to a noumenon (a value judgment) and not a phenomenon (a discernible factual situation). By the use of the word 'safe', safe from what? Safe from the indignation and reproaches of the convicted person and those campaigning on his behalf? Or ought we to have the sense of the verdict being *secure* (or impregnable) against any critical forensic analysis by academics, armchair critics, logical or factual in their criticisms? What about dipping into the Thesaurus and coming up with analogues, such as unassailable, water-tight, certain, well-founded, solidly based, reliable, incontrovertible, or conclusive? To truncate this excursion into the realms of lexicography, I would prefer 'unsatisfactory', which is a good word to encompass anything ranging from 'there's a strong smell of doubt about this verdict' to 'the lurking doubt' formula much favoured by some past members of the judiciary.

It is with some amusement that one notices that the Scottish Committee on Criminal Appeals and Miscarriages of Justice Procedures (the Sutherland Committee, HMSO 3245, June 1996) recommended that the general basis for a successful appeal in Scotland under section 228(2), Criminal Procedure (Scotland) Act 1975, should remain that 'a miscarriage of justice' has occurred, and that this ground should not be qualified or limited in any way. The Committee specifically did not favour the concept of a conviction being 'unsafe', as enacted in England. So the search for a satisfactory formula continues along different routes in each system.

The Sutherland Committee joined hands with the Runciman Commission and Parliament in favouring an independent body with powers to refer cases of miscarriage of justice to the appeal court. If England and Wales (including Northern Ireland) had an independent Criminal Cases Review Commission (as established in Part II of the Criminal Appeal Act 1995), then Scotland should, it would appear, have no less. After a careful consideration of the options available for public response for handling claims of miscarriage of justice in the criminal process – a good deal more thought than was given to the topic by the Runciman Commission – the Sutherland Committee opted for a replication in miniature (due to the scale of the problem in Scotland). It did so because of the need to preserve the separation of powers between executive authority and the judiciary. An independent body detached from any political influence was indicated. Sadly, the story does not end there. On the day of the publication of the Sutherland Committee report, the Secretary of State for Scotland, Mr Michael Forsyth, announced the Government's rejection of the recommendation for an independent review body. Despite the political union, Scottish and English criminal justice systems continue to tread their different paths.

Louis Blom-Cooper

Introduction

The motivation behind this statute needs little explanation. Throughout the last ten to 15 years, there has been an unremitting campaign by numerous organisations and individuals for an improved criminal appeals system. Many have been concerned with specific cases such as the Birmingham Six and the Guildford Four, whereas others have criticised the system in a wider context. This widespread concern, among other things, resulted in the institution of the Royal Commission on Criminal Justice in 1991 which reported its findings two years later. The current legislation, which received the Royal Assent in July 1995, largely reflects the recommendations of the Royal Commission headed by Lord Runciman.

As one can imagine, this statute had a chequered passage through Parliament and attracted many amendments. For example, one inclusion, to make a provision which would have provided persons sentenced to mandatory life with the right to appeal to the Court of Appeal against the minimum prison term recommended by the trial judge to the Home Secretary, was rejected on the grounds that it would cause anomalies.

Much of the Criminal Appeal Act affects Northern Ireland as well as England and Wales and therefore extensive reference is made to the relevant Northern Ireland legislation.

PART I

The Court of Appeal

Leave to Appeal

1.1 Section 1(1) of the Criminal Appeal Act 1995 ('the 1995 Act') substitutes a new s. 1(2) into the Criminal Appeal Act 1968 ('the 1968 Act'), which now provides that an appeal to the Court of Appeal (Criminal Division) against a conviction for an offence tried on indictment, may only be made if the trial judge grants a certificate that the case is fit for appeal, or with the leave of the Court of Appeal. The original s. 1(2) (a) of the 1968 Act gave an automatic right of appeal on any ground which involved a question of law alone but this no longer applies.

1.2 The new provisions therefore require that leave is obtained from the Court of Appeal or a certificate obtained from the trial judge in respect of *all* appeals regardless of whether they are based upon a question of law, fact, mixed law and fact, or any other ground.

1.3 The same principles under s. 1(1) as explained in 1.1 and 1.2 above, apply to subsections (2) to (6) below which amend the earlier provisions where shown in brackets:

(2) The Criminal Appeal (Northern Ireland) Act 1980 ('the 1980 Act') s. 1 (appeal against conviction in Northern Ireland).

(3) Section 12 of the 1968 Act (appeal against insanity verdict).

(4) Section 12(1) of the 1980 Act (appeal against insanity verdict in Northern Ireland).

(5) Section 15(2) of the 1968 Act (appeal against finding of disability [ie unfitness to plead]).

(6) Section 13A(2) of the 1980 Act (appeal in Northern Ireland against finding of unfitness to be tried).

Grounds for Allowing and Dismissing Appeals

2.1 Section 2(1) of the 1995 Act substitutes a new s. 2(1) into the 1968 Act by providing that the Court of Appeal shall either allow an appeal against conviction if they think that the conviction is unsafe or shall dismiss the appeal in any other case. In the past, convictions were quashed on the grounds that the original conviction was considered to be unsafe and unsatisfactory. The omission of the word 'unsatisfactory' is probably because it is considered superfluous. According to Professor Zander (*Cases and Materials on the English Legal System* (6th ed., Butterworths), 1993), during the final appeal of the Birmingham Six it was submitted that convictions could be safe even if they were unsatisfactory, thereby subscribing that the two words had different meanings. This argument was rejected by the Court of Appeal which took the view that they both had the same meaning. It would therefore seem that the 1995 Act has omitted the word 'unsatisfactory' for the avoidance of doubt.

2.2 The same principles under s. 2(1), as explained in 2.1 above, apply to subsections (2) to (6) below which amend the earlier provisions where shown in brackets:

(2) Section 2(1) of the 1980 Act (disposal of appeal against conviction in Northern Ireland).
(3) Section 13(1) and (2) of the 1968 Act (disposal of appeal against insanity verdict).
(4) Section 12(2) and (3) of the 1980 Act (appeal against insanity verdict in Northern Ireland).
(5) Section 16(1) of the 1968 Act (disposal of appeal against finding of disability).
(6) Section 13A(3) and (4) of the 1980 Act (appeal in Northern Ireland against finding of unfitness to be tried).

Abolition of References by the Home Secretary

3.1 Section 3 of the 1995 Act repeals s. 17 of the 1968 Act and s. 14 of the 1980 Act, whereby the Home Secretary had the power to refer a case to the Court of Appeal following a conviction on indictment or a finding of insanity or unfitness to plead, or to seek an opinion from the Court of Appeal. However, provision is made under the 1995 Act for the new Criminal Cases Review Commission to perform this task in future (see Part II below).

Evidence

4.1 Section 4 of the 1995 Act substitutes a number of new provisions under s. 23 of the 1968 Act and s. 25 of the 1980 Act. Section 4(1) (a) substitutes a new paragraph (c) under s. 23 subsection (1) of the 1968 Act (power to receive evidence etc). This means that the Court of Appeal may receive any *evidence* which was not adduced in the earlier proceedings whereas the earlier provision generally allowed it to receive the evidence of any *witness*.

4.2 Section 4(1) (b) replaces subsection (2) under s.23 (duty to receive evidence in certain circumstances), so that the Court of Appeal shall have regard to the following when considering whether to receive any evidence:

(a) whether the evidence appears to be 'capable of belief' (the earlier provision used the wording 'likely to be credible').
(b) whether it appears that the evidence may give any ground for allowing the appeal.
(c) whether the evidence on an issue which is the subject of the appeal would have been admissible in the earlier proceedings, and
(d) whether the failure to adduce the evidence in the earlier proceedings can be reasonably explained.

4.3 Section 4(1) (c) amends subsection (3) under s. 23 which now means that the Court of Appeal may receive any evidence that was not adduced in the earlier proceedings (see 4.1 above), and this applies to any evidence of a witness (including the appellant) who is competent but not compellable. This also applies to the appellant's spouse where the appellant makes an application for that purpose and the evidence could not have been given in the earlier proceedings without that application.

4.4 Section 4(2) (a), (b) and (c) substitute identical provisions in subsections (1) (c), (2) and (3) under s. 25 of the 1980 Act as in 4.1, 4.2 and 4.3 above.

Power to Order Investigations

5.1 Section 5(1) inserts a new s. 23A into the 1968 Act which provides that where a case comes before the Court of Appeal, it may direct the proposed Criminal Cases Review Commission ('the Commission') to investigate and report to it on any matter which ought to be resolved before the appeal is decided. These investigations should be confined to matters which cannot be resolved by the court and are likely to enable the court to resolve the issue.

5.2 Subsections (2), (3) and (4) to the new s. 23A insert a number of procedural measures applicable to these investigations. These provide that directions by the Court of Appeal under 5.1 above shall be in writing and shall specify the matter to be investigated, copies of which shall be given to the appellant and the respondent who shall, at the outset, be given the Commission's report plus any statements, opinions and other reports attached to it.

5.3 Section 5 Subsection (2) to the 1995 Act inserts a new s. 25A into the 1980 Act which contains identical provisions to those described in 5.1 and 5.2 above, thereby bringing these functions of the Commission in criminal appeals in Northern Ireland into line with the provisions applicable to England and Wales.

Powers exercisable by the registrar

6.1 Section 6 of the 1995 Act inserts a new s. 31A into the 1968 Act which provides under subsections (1) and (2) that the registrar may do the following on behalf of the Court of Appeal:

(a) extend the time limit within which notice of appeal or application for leave to appeal may be given.
(b) order a witness to attend the hearing for examination.
(c) vary the conditions of bail granted to an appellant by the Crown Court or the Court of Appeal.

6.2 Subsection (3) states that the registrar may not vary the appellant's conditions of bail if the respondent objects.

6.3 By subsection (4), if, on application by the appellant, the registrar refuses to exercise any of the above powers in his favour, the appellant shall be entitled to have the application determined by a single judge.

Appeals in Cases of Death

7.1 Section 7(1) of the 1995 Act inserts a new s. 44A into the 1968 Act and provides that if an appellant dies before or during a criminal appeal (including an appeal commenced by virtue of a reference to the Criminal Cases Review Commission), a person approved by the Court of Appeal may either begin an appeal or continue it in place of the deceased, but an application must be made within a year of the death. However, this time limit will not apply where a case for an appeal was begun by a reference to the Criminal Cases Review Commission.

7.2 The persons whom the Court of Appeal may approve for the purposes of 7.1 may only be the deceased's widow or widower, a person who is the personal representative as defined under s. 55(1)(xi) of the Administration of Estates Act 1925, or any other person who appears to the Court of Appeal to have a substantial financial or other interest in the outcome of a criminal appeal by virtue of a family or similar relationship.

7.3 The power to approve a person under 7.2 will be exercised by a single judge although the applicant will be entitled to have the matter decided by the Court of Appeal in the event of a refusal.

7.4 Section 7(2) of the 1995 Act inserts a new s. 47A into the 1980 Act pertaining to Northern Ireland. Basically the new provisions affecting Northern Ireland are the same as those described in 7.1, 7.2 and 7.3 but with the following exceptions:

(a) A personal representative is defined under the Wills and Administration Proceedings (Northern Ireland) Order 1994, and
(b) There is no specific mention of provisions mentioned in 7.3 applicable to Northern Ireland.

PART II

The Criminal Cases Review Commission

The Commission

8.1 Section 8(1) of the 1995 Act provides for the institution of the Criminal Cases Review Commission ('the Commission') which will be a body corporate and will not be part of the Crown [subsection (2)]. No fewer than 11 persons shall be in the Commission [subsection (3)], and each will be appointed by the Queen on the recommendation of the Prime Minister [subsection (4)]. According to recently published material, the new body will be based in Birmingham.

8.2 At least one-third of the Commission shall be legally qualified although such persons must either be barristers or solicitors holding a ten-year general qualification under the Courts and Legal Services Act 1990 [subsection (5) (a)], or have at least ten-years' standing as a member of the Bar of Northern Ireland, or as a solicitor of the Supreme Court of Northern Ireland [subsection (5) (b)].

8.3 At least two-thirds of the Commission shall have expertise in the criminal justice system, particularly within the ambit of criminal investigations and the treatment of offenders, including at least one who has knowledge or experience of this subject in Northern Ireland [subsection (6)].

Schedule 1

8.4 Section 8 ends by giving effect to Schedule 1 which enacts further provisions with regard to the new Commission [subsection (7)].

8.5 Under Schedule 1, the chairperson of the new Commission will be appointed by the Queen on the recommendation of the

Prime Minister.* This Schedule then goes on to provide the following terms applicable to members of the Commission including the chairperson.

8.6 Members of the Commission may be either full or part-time, and members (including the chairperson) will be appointed for a fixed five-year term which is renewable. (Recent recruitment material indicates that three-year terms will also be considered.) This will only be done once since no member shall hold office for a continuous period of more than ten years. However, a member may resign at any time during their term in office.

8.7 A member of the Commission may be removed at any time if that person has failed, without reasonable excuse, to discharge his or her functions for three continuous months, or has been convicted of a criminal offence, or if he or she is involved in certain bankruptcy proceedings, or is generally unfit to function as a member.

8.8 Schedule 1 goes on to make various provisions regarding the remuneration of members of the Commission. These include fees, allowances, expenses, pensions and compensation where appropriate. Provision is also made for the appointment of a chief executive and other employees by the Commission.

8.9 The Commission may determine for itself the procedures it wishes to adopt including the quorum for meetings. However, there is one proviso under Schedule 1 whereby the following functions must be performed by a committee of at least three members:

(a) Making references to the courts under any of sections 9 to 12 of the 1995 Act (see 9.1 to 9.3, 10.1, 11.1 to 11.4 and 12.1 below).
(b) Reporting to the Court of Appeal under s. 15(4) of the 1995 Act (see 15.3 below).
(c) Providing the Home Secretary with a statement under s. 16(1) (b) of the 1995 Act (see 16.1 below).
(d) The appointment of an investigating officer under s. 19 of the 1995 Act (see 19.1 to 19.5 below).

* Sir Frederick Crawford (formerly Vice-Chancellor of Aston University) has recently been appointed as chairperson.

With regard to documents where disclosure may be contrary to the interests of national security, the Commission are under a duty to deal with such documents so as not to endanger those interests.

8.10 Schedule 1 concludes by making various provisions in respect of the Commission's general accountability. These include submitting an annual report on its activities to the Home Secretary which in turn is to be laid before both Houses of Parliament, and also the submission of its accounts to the Home Secretary and the Comptroller and Auditor General.

References to Court

9.1 Section 9 of the 1995 Act concerns cases dealt with on indictment in England and Wales, and provides the Commission with the power to refer convictions at any time to the Court of Appeal. Even if they do not refer the conviction, they may at any time refer any sentence to the Court of Appeal. However, this does not apply where the sentence is fixed by law, namely, mandatory life.

9.2 References by the Commission in respect of conviction will be treated the same as an appeal by a convicted person in accordance with Section 1 of the 1968 Act; references by the Commission regarding sentence will similarly be treated as an appeal by the person convicted but in accordance with s. 9 of the 1968 Act.

9.3 Section 9 of the 1995 Act goes on to provide the Commission with powers to refer cases at any time to the Court of Appeal involving not guilty by reason of insanity verdicts. Such references will be treated as an appeal by the person in accordance with s. 12 of the 1968 Act. Finally, in cases of unfitness to plead where a jury determines that a person was under a disability (unfit to plead) and did the act or made the omission charged, the Commission may at any time refer one or both of these findings to the Court of Appeal. This will be treated as an appeal by the person against whom these findings were made in accordance with s. 15 of the 1968 Act.

Cases Dealt With on Indictment in Northern Ireland

10.1 The provisions under s. 10 of the 1995 Act which apply to Northern Ireland are almost identical to those under s. 9 which are applicable to England and Wales. These are explained in 9.1, 9.2 and 9.3 above, but with the following exceptions:

(a) Subsection (5) states that on a reference by the Commission in respect of conviction or sentence, the Court of Appeal may not impose a sentence more severe than that passed by the Crown Court. No such specific requirement has been made under s. 9.

(b) Appropriate references in this section are made to the 1980 Act.

Cases Dealt With Summarily in England and Wales

11.1 Section 11 of the 1995 Act provides that where a person has been convicted of an offence by a magistrates' court in England and Wales (namely, a summary offence or one which is triable either way), the Commission may at any time refer the conviction to the Crown Court. It may also refer any sentence imposed by magistrates to the Crown Court at any time, even if they have not referred the conviction [subsection (1)].

11.2 References by the Commission under 11.1 above shall be treated as appeals by the person under s. 108(1) of the Magistrates' Courts Act 1980. Where the reference is against conviction, it is irrelevant whether or not a plea of guilty was made [subsection (2)].

11.3 Provision is made under s. 11(6) of the 1995 Act that, on a reference by the Commission, the Crown Court may not impose a penalty more severe than that originally awarded by the magistrates' court. This is in contrast to the rules which apply when an *appellant* makes an appeal. In such cases the Crown Court may increase the original sentence provided it does not exceed the maximum sentencing powers held by magistrates [s. 48(1) and (4) of the Supreme Court Act 1981].

11.4 Section 11 ends by stating that the Crown Court may grant bail to persons whose conviction or sentence have been referred by the Commission, but any time on bail will not count towards any custodial sentence [subsection (7)].

Cases Dealt With Summarily in Northern Ireland

12.1 Section 12 of the 1995 Act which applies to Northern Ireland makes very similar provisions to s. 11 applicable to England and Wales as covered in 11.1, 11.2, 11.3 and 11.4 above, although there are some significant differences as follows:

(a) Any reference by the Commission against conviction or sentence by magistrates is to be made to a *county* court.

(b) The granting of any bail to persons whose conviction or sentence have been referred by the Commission will be made by the *High Court*.

(c) Appropriate references in this section are made to Article 140(1) of the Magistrates' Courts (Northern Ireland) Order 1981.

Conditions for Making of References

13.1 Section 13 of the 1995 Act makes a number of provisos regarding references by the Commission. Subsection (1) (a) provides that references pertaining to convictions, verdicts, findings or sentences shall not be made under sections 9 to 12, unless the Commission considers that there is a real possibility of a successful appeal against the original decision.

13.2 Subsection (1) (c) adds that such references may also not be made unless appeals against convictions, verdicts, findings or sentences have been determined, or leave to appeal against any of these has been refused. However, subsection (2) enables the Commission to make a reference if there are exceptional circumstances which justify it.

13.3 Subsection (1) (b) (i) provides that references by the Commission, in the case of convictions, verdicts or findings (but not sentences), shall not be made if any argument or evidence was raised in any earlier proceedings leading to it [except under exceptional circumstances as provided under subsection (2)].

13.4 In the case of sentences only, subsection (1) (b) (ii) provides that references by the Commission shall not be made unless an argument on a point of law or information was also not raised in earlier proceedings. Note, however, that there is no provision for the waiving of this restriction in 'exceptional circumstances' under subsection (2).

Further Provisions about References

14.1 Further provisions are made under s. 14 with regard to references by the Commission. Subsection (1) provides that references under sections 9 to 12 pertaining to convictions, verdicts, findings or sentences may be made after an application has been made by or on behalf of the person concerned, or without the making of an application.

14.2 Subsection (2) states that the Commission, when considering whether to make references of convictions, verdicts, findings or sentences under sections 9 to 12, shall take into account any applications or representations made to it by or on behalf of the person concerned, or any other representations and other relevant matters.

14.3 With regard to references under sections 9 or 10, subsection (3) provides that where the Commission is considering making such references, it may at any time seek an opinion of the Court of Appeal on any point and the Court shall give its opinion to the Commission accordingly.

14.4 Subsection (4) covers certain procedural matters relating to references made by the Commission under sections 9 to 12. Where such a reference is made, the Commission must provide a statement of its reasons to the court dealing with it, and a copy should be sent to every party likely to be involved in the subsequent appeal proceedings.

14.5 Subsection (5) provides that where references by the Commission under sections 9 to 12 are treated as appeals against convictions, verdicts, findings or sentences, the appeal may be on any ground which need not necessarily be related to any reason given by the Commission for making the reference.

14.6 Where an application is made to the Commission for a reference under sections 9 to 12 but it decides not to proceed, subsection (6) provides that the Commission shall provide a statement of their reasons to the applicant.

Investigations and Assistance

Investigations for Court of Appeal

15.1 Section 15(1) makes provision with regard to investigations on behalf of the Court of Appeal. Where the Court of Appeal gives a direction under the new s. 23(A) (1) of the 1968 Act and the new s. 25(A) (1) of the 1980 Act (see 5.1 and 5.3 above), the Commission has the discretion to investigate the matter as it thinks fit.

15.2 Under s. 15(2), where the Commission is investigating a matter under a direction by the Court of Appeal, the Commission has the power to investigate any other matter which arises and is relevant to the determination of the case. The term 'related matter' is used in the Act to describe this.

15.3 Section 15(3), (4), (5), (6) and (7) provides that the Commission has a duty to keep the Court of Appeal informed of the progress of all matters under investigation (including any 'related matter'), and shall report their investigations when they have been completed, or beforehand if requested by the Court of Appeal. These reports should be accompanied by any statements, opinions and reports relevant to the investigation although these do not have to include reports by investigating officers under s. 20(6) (see 20.2 below).

Assistance in Connection with the Prerogative of Mercy

16.1 The Royal Prerogative of Mercy is these days exercised by the Home Secretary on behalf of the Queen, although it is more commonly known as a free pardon. The effect of a pardon is to wipe out a criminal conviction and its consequences, although it does not quash or overturn a conviction in the same way as the

Court of Appeal. Section 16(1) empowers the Home Secretary to seek the advice of the Commission when considering a pardon. This section ends with the following statement: '. . . and the Secretary of State shall, in considering whether so to recommend, treat the Commission's statement as conclusive of the matter referred'. This implies that the Commission's views when sought, given in a statement containing their conclusions, will constitute the final word on the matter being decided, prior to the Home Secretary making his decision.

16.2 Section 16(2) states that where the Commission are of the opinion that the Home Secretary should consider whether to recommend a free pardon in any case, they shall give him their reasons accordingly.

Power to Obtain Documents etc.

17.1 Section 17 concerns documents and other material held by persons within public bodies which may assist the Commission in any of their duties. A 'public body' is defined under s. 22(1) (see 22.1 below) as:

- (a) any police force,
- (b) any government department, local authority or other body constituted for the purposes of the public service, local government or the administration of justice, or
- (c) any other body whose members are appointed by Her Majesty, any minister or any government department or whose revenues consist wholly or mainly of money provided by Parliament or apppropriated by Measure of the Northern Ireland Assembly.

17.2 Under s. 17(2), where it is reasonable to do so the Commission may require the 'appropriate person' (see 17.4 below) within the relevant public body, to produce or give the Commission access to the document or material and to allow them to remove or copy it. Furthermore, the Commission may direct the appropriate person to preserve such documents or other material until the direction is withdrawn. This means that they must not be destroyed, damaged or altered unless the Commission authorise it.

17.3 Under subsection (4) the above duties by public bodies must be complied with regardless of whether the document or material is secret or generally classified by virtue of any legal limitation.

17.4 The term 'appropriate person' is defined under s. 22(4) below as follows (see also 22.4):

(a) a chief officer of a police force
(b) the Director of Public Prosecutions
(c) the Director of Public Prosecutions for Northern Ireland
(d) the Director of the Serious Fraud Office
(e) the Commissioners of Inland Revenue
(f) the Commissioners of Customs and Excise
(g) the Minister in charge of any other government department
(h) any other public body itself if it is a body corporate, or the person in charge of any other public body if it is not a body corporate.

Documents etc. Relating to Current or Old Cases

18.1 Section 18 provides that s. 17 above does not apply to documents or materials held by officials in a government department where this information is in their possession or control as a result of the Home Secretary's consideration of the case. This applies to cases which are being considered by the Home Secretary for either a reference or the exercise of the prerogative of mercy regarding a conviction by a magistrates' court immediately prior to the date on which s. 17 comes into force, or if the Home Secretary has considered such a case at any earlier date. However, provision is made for such information to be provided to the Commission by the Home Secretary himself except documents and materials received from government officials.

Power to Require Appointment of Investigating Officers

19.1 Section 19(1) provides the Commission with the power to initiate the appointment of investigating officers in order to assist in any of their cases which require such assistance.

19.2 Subsection (2) states that where any offence to which such cases apply was investigated by a person serving in a 'public body' (see 22.1 below), the 'appropriate person' within that organisation (see 22.4 below) may be required under subsection (5) to appoint someone within that public body to act as investigating officer. Alternatively, someone serving in a police force or a person within another public body which has investigating functions may be appointed. Subsection (2) goes on to provide that where the public body no longer exists, the appointment of an investigating officer will fall upon any chief officer of police or upon the appropriate person of any public body which has functions, in whole or part, which are similar to that former body.

19.3 Where no offence was investigated by persons within a public body, subsection (3) provides that the requirement to appoint an investigating officer will fall upon any chief officer of police who, under subsection (4), may either be an officer within his own force or selected from another police force.

19.4 Subsection (6) states that the Commission may direct that their approval be sought regarding the appointment of a person, or the selection of a police force or other public body under subsections (4) and (5).

19.5 Subsection (7) provides that the appointment of investigating officers by appropriate persons within public bodies shall be notified to the Commission. If they are dissatisfied, the Commission may direct the appropriate person to select another investigator and to notify them when a replacement has been made as soon as is reasonably practicable. The other person shall not be appointed without the Commission's approval.

Inquiries by Investigating Officers

20.1 Section 20(1), (2) and (4) provide that persons appointed as investigating officers shall undertake such inquiries as the Commission may reasonably direct, who in turn may take appropriate steps to supervise the investigating officer. Also, the appropriate person within the public body where an investigating officer is serving shall permit the investigator to act as such.

20.2 Subsections (5), (6) and (7) provide that the Commission may at any time remove an investigating officer from a case and replace him under their powers under s. 19. On the completion of a case, an investigating officer shall prepare and submit a report of his findings to the Commission (including any statements, opinions and other reports), and a copy of the report shall be sent to the person who appointed him.

20.3 Subsection (3) states that where a member of the Royal Ulster Constabulary is appointed as an investigator by a chief police officer within England and Wales, that investigator shall have the same powers within England and Wales as if he were a constable there, and vice versa.

Other Powers

21.1 Section 21 provides that nothing in sections 17 to 20 shall prevent the Commission from taking any steps considered appropriate in the exercise of their functions. This will include, in particular, undertaking, or arranging for others to undertake, inquiries, and to obtain statements, opinions and reports.

Meaning of 'Public Body' etc.

22.1 Section 22 defines and clarifies several key terms used in the 1995 Act namely 'public body', 'police force' (and 'chief officer of police'), 'government department', 'Minister', and 'appropriate person'. The term 'public body' has been mentioned above under sections 17, 19 and 20 (see 17.1 to 17.3, 19.2 to 19.5 and 20.1), and is repeated here for clarification. Section 22(1) defines a 'public body' as follows:

(a) any police force,
(b) any government department, local authority or other body constituted for the purposes of the public service, local government or the administration of justice, or
(c) any other body whose members are appointed by Her Majesty, any Minister or any government department or

whose revenues consist wholly or mainly of money provided by Parliament or appropriated by Measure of the Northern Ireland Assembly.

22.2 The term 'police force' is mentioned in sections 19 and 20 above (see 19.2 to 19.4 and also 20.3). Subsection (2) states that:

(a) a 'police force' includes the Royal Ulster Constabulary and the Royal Ulster Constabulary Reserve and any body of constables maintained otherwise than by a police authority,
(b) references to the chief officer of police in relation to the Royal Ulster Constabulary and the Royal Ulster Constabulary Reserve, are the Chief Constable of the Constabulary and, in relation to a police force maintained otherwise than by a police authority, the chief constable, and
(c) references to an England and Wales police force are to a police force maintained under s. 2 of the Police Act 1964, the metropolitan police force or the City of London police force.

22.3 Subsection (3) states that reference to a 'government department' under s. 18 above (see 18.1) includes a Northern Ireland department and the Office of the Director of Public Prosecutions for Northern Ireland. The term 'Minister' means a Minister of the Crown defined under s. 8 of the Ministers of the Crown Act 1975. This includes the head of a Northern Ireland department.

22.4 The term 'appropriate person' is mentioned in sections 17, 19 and 20 above (see 17.2, 17.4, 19.2, 19.5 and 20.1), and is repeated here for clarification. Subsection (4) defines an 'appropriate person' as:

(a) a chief officer of police
(b) the Director of Public Prosecutions
(c) the Director of Public Prosecutions for Northern Ireland
(d) the Director of the Serious Fraud Office
(e) the Commissioners of Inland Revenue
(f) the Commissioners of Customs & Excise
(g) the Minister in charge of any other government department
(h) any other public body itself if it is a body corporate, or the person in charge of any other public body if it is not a body corporate.

22.5 Subsection (5) clarifies two points pertaining to sections 17, 19 and 20 above. First, a justices' chief executive or justices' clerk who has been appointed by a magistrates' courts committee or is a member of staff there, shall be treated as serving in that committee. Second, anyone authorised under s. 57 of the Northern Ireland (Emergency Provisions) Act 1991 to exercise powers under Schedule 5 shall be treated as if he were both serving in a public body and were also the appropriate person. Section 57 of the 1991 Act empowers superintendents and above in the Royal Ulster Constabulary to request the Secretary of State to appoint civilian experts, such as accountants, to assist in the investigation of the resources of proscribed organisations. These civilian investigators are given certain investigative powers under Schedule 5 to the 1991 Act including the power to apply for search warrants. (See also the Proceeds of Crime [Northern Ireland] Order 1996 [1996 No. 1299 (NI9)] due to take effect on 25 August 1996.)

Disclosure of Information

Offence of Disclosure

23.1 Section 23(1) and (2) states that past or present members or employees of the Criminal Cases Review Commission or investigating officers shall not disclose information obtained in the course of their functions unless excepted by s. 24 (see 24.1 below).

23.2 Subsection (3) provides that no member of the Commission shall authorise the disclosure of any information obtained in the exercise of its functions by an employee of the Commission or an investigating officer unless excepted by s. 24.

23.3 Subsection (4) creates the offence of unauthorised disclosure which is punishable on summary conviction by a fine not exceeding level five on the standard scale (currently £5,000).

Exceptions from Obligations of Non-Disclosure

24.1 Under s. 24(1), the disclosure of information or its authorisation is excepted from s. 23 (see 23.1 and 23.2 above) if the information is:

(a) for the purposes of any criminal, disciplinary or civil proceedings.
(b) to assist in dealing with an application for compensation for a miscarriage of justice.
(c) a transfer of information between employees and members of the Commission and investigating officers.
(d) any statement, report or other information required in the exercise of any function under the 1995 Act.
(e) any information which may be disclosed by order of the Home Secretary. Under subsection (5) the power to make such an order will be through statutory instrument which shall be subject to annulment by either House in Parliament.

Subsection (4) states that the above information is not prevented from disclosure by virtue of any obligation of secrecy or other legal limitation.

24.2 Subsection (2) provides a further exception to the restrictions under s. 23 where the information is disclosed by an employee of the Commission or an investigating officer who has been authorised by a member of the Commission to do so.

Subsection (4) provides that the above information is not prevented from disclosure by virtue of any obligation of secrecy or other legal restriction.

24.3 Subsection (3) states that unless any disclosure would run contrary to an obligation of secrecy or other legal limitation, other exceptions to s. 23 will include disclosure for the purposes of a criminal investigation or in deciding upon a prosecution.

Consent to Disclosure

25.1 Section 25 affects persons who are required to submit or preserve information in accordance with s. 17 above (see 17.1 to 17.4). Section 25(1) provides that where a person has such a requirement imposed upon him under s. 17 and he notifies the Commission that they may not disclose the contents of that information, the Commission shall not disclose it without that person's consent.

25.2 Subsection (2), however, states that such consent may not be withheld (apart from s. 17) unless that person would have been prevented by any obligation of secrecy or other legal restriction on disclosure, and it is reasonable for that person to withhold his consent.

25.3 Subsection (3) removes the justification for withholding consent under subsection (2) (a) where such restriction is contingent upon another's authorisation, unless reasonable steps have been taken to obtain such authorisation or it could not reasonably be expected to be obtained.

PART III

Other Provisions

Powers of Magistrates' Courts to Rectify Mistakes

Extension of Power of Courts in England and Wales

26.1 Section 26 of the 1995 Act makes several amendments to s. 142 of the Magistrates' Courts Act 1980. First, s. 142(1) of the 1980 Act is amended so that 'a magistrates' court may vary or rescind a sentence or other order imposed or made by it when dealing with an offender if it appears to the court to be in the interests of justice to do so'. The earlier provisions were subject to subsection (4) of s. 142 (now repealed) which imposed a time limit of 28 days, and made provisos regarding the composition of the court during such proceedings. The original provisions also did not include the present requirement that such proceedings should be in the interests of justice.

26.2 Section 26(3) of the 1995 Act inserts a new (1A) under s. 142(1) of the 1980 Act which states that the power of the magistrates' court under subsection (1) (see 26.1 above) cannot be exercised if the Crown Court has determined an appeal against that or any sentence or order or the conviction itself, or if the High Court has determined a case stated regarding those proceedings.

26.3 Section 26(4) of the 1995 Act amends s. 142(2) of the 1980 Act which makes provision for a case tried summarily to be reheard by a different panel of magistrates where a defendant has been found guilty and it is in the interests of justice to do so. The amendments merely simplify the wording of the first part and remove the requirement that this is subject to s. 142(4).

26.4 Section 26(5) of the 1995 Act inserts a new (2A) under s. 142(2) which states that the power of the magistrates' court under subsection (2) (see 26.3 above) cannot be exercised if the Crown Court has determined an appeal against the conviction or any sentence or order imposed, or the High Court has determined a case stated in respect of those proceedings.

26.5 Section 26(6) of the 1995 Act effects a small change to the wording of s. 142(3) of the 1980 Act by substituting the word 'conviction' for the words 'finding of guilty' as originally used in s. 142(3) (a).

26.6 Section 26(7) of the 1995 Act repeals s. 142(4) of the 1980 Act which imposed a time limit of 28 days upon the proceedings covered under the original subsections (1) and (2), and in both cases stipulated the composition of the court accordingly.

Introduction of Power in Northern Ireland

27.1 Section 27 of the 1995 Act inserts a new s. 158A into the Magistrates' Courts (Northern Ireland) Order 1981 which effectively brings the provisions of the 1981 Act in line with the changes effected under s. 26 of the 1995 Act with regard to the powers of magistrates' courts to rectify mistakes (see 26.1 to 26.6 above). There are, however, some minor differences. Under the Northern Ireland provisions, the power of magistrates' courts to re-open cases to rectify mistakes under the new s. 158A(1) cannot be exercised if the county court has determined an appeal in respect of the case or the Court of Appeal has determined a case stated, whereas in England and Wales it will be the Crown Court and High Court respectively. This also applies to the new s. 158A(3).

Compensation for Miscarriages of Justice

Assessment of Compensation

28.1 Section 28 of the 1995 Act inserts a new subsection (4A) under s. 133 of the Criminal Justice Act 1988. The following is a summary of the existing and new provisions.

Under s. 133(1) to (7), if a person is convicted of a criminal offence where sentence is subsequently passed and his conviction is later reversed or he receives a pardon on the ground that there has been a miscarriage of justice, the Home Secretary shall pay compensation accordingly. This is contingent upon an application being made to the Home Secretary for compensation and also whether the new fact resulting in the quashing of the conviction or the giving of the pardon was attributable to non-disclosure on the part of the person convicted. However, the Home Secretary has the power to determine whether there is a right to compensation in all cases.

28.2 Compensation shall be paid to the person who has suffered punishment (namely, received sentence), or his personal representatives if he is dead, and the amount of any compensation shall be assessed by a person appointed by the Home Secretary to act as an assessor. This latter provision comes under subsection (4) which is effectively extended by the new subsection (4A) which states that the assessor shall particularly take into account the seriousness of the offence, the severity of the punishment, the conduct of the investigation and prosecution, and any other convictions and subsequent punishments attributable to the applicant. The new subsection (4A) also extends the suffering of punishment to include harm to reputation or similar damage.

PART IV

Supplementary

Minor and Consequential Amendments and Repeals

29.1 Section 29 generally gives effect to Schedule 2 to the 1995 Act and gives guidance regarding Schedule 3.

Interpretation

30.1 Section 30 interprets a number of references, the most significant of which are covered in the commentary.

Financial Provisions

31.1 Section 31 generally provides that any expenditure incurred by the Home Secretary, with regard to the Criminal Cases Review Commission, shall be paid out of money provided by Parliament.

Commencement

32.1 Section 32 states that the 1995 Act shall take effect by statutory instrument on such day as the Home Secretary may order. Note that SI 1995/3061 enabled the following sections of the 1995 Act to commence on 1 January 1996: sections 1, 2, 4, 6, 7, 26, 27, 28, 29, 30, 31, 32, 33 and 34; and also Schedules 2 and 3.

Extent

33.1 Section 33 basically states the extent to which certain parts of the 1995 Act apply to England and Wales or to Northern Ireland.

Short Title

34.1 Section 34 states that this Act will be known as the Criminal Appeal Act 1995.

Schedules

Schedule 1. The Commission

The main provisions under Schedule 1 have been incorporated in the commentary covering the Criminal Cases Review Commission under Part II (see 8.3 to 8.9 above).

Schedule 2. Minor and Consequential Amendments

Schedule 2 makes a number of minor and consequential changes to different statutes.

Schedule 3. Repeals

Schedule 3 lists statutory provisions repealed by the 1995 Act.

Criminal Appeal Act 1995
(19 July 1995)

PART I

THE COURT OF APPEAL

1.—(1) In the Criminal Appeal Act 1968 ("the 1968 Act"), in section 1 (appeal against conviction), for subsection (2) (requirement of leave to appeal or certificate of trial judge unless appeal involves question of law only) substitute— Leave to appeal etc. 1968 c. 19.

"(2) An appeal under this section lies only—

(a) with the leave of the Court of Appeal; or
(b) if the judge of the court of trial grants a certificate that the case is fit for appeal."

(2) In the Criminal Appeal (Northern Ireland) Act 1980 ("the 1980 Act"), in section 1 (appeal against conviction subject to requirement of leave to appeal or certificate of trial judge unless appeal involves question of law only), for the words from "conviction" to the end substitute "conviction— 1980 c. 47.

(a) with the leave of the Court; or
(b) if the judge of the court of trial grants a certificate that the case is fit for appeal."

(3) In section 12 of the 1968 Act (appeal against verdict of not guilty by reason of insanity subject to requirement of leave to appeal or certificate of trial judge unless appeal involves question of law only), for the words from "against the verdict" to the end substitute "against the verdict—

(a) with the leave of the Court of Appeal; or
(b) if the judge of the court of trial grants a certificate that the case is fit for appeal."

(4) In section 12(1) of the 1980 Act (appeal against finding of not guilty on ground of insanity subject to requirement of leave to

appeal or certificate of trial judge unless appeal involves question of law only), for the words from "against that finding" to the end substitute "to the Court of Appeal against the finding—

(a) with the leave of the Court; or

(b) if the judge of the court of trial grants a certificate that the case is fit for appeal."

(5) In section 15 of the 1968 Act (appeal against finding of disability), for subsection (2) (requirement of leave to appeal or certificate of trial judge unless appeal involves question of law only) substitute—

"(2) An appeal under this section lies only—

(a) with the leave of the Court of Appeal; or

(b) if the judge of the court of trial grants a certificate that the case is fit for appeal."

(6) In section 13A of the 1980 Act (appeal against finding of unfitness to be tried), for subsection (2) (requirement of leave to appeal or certificate of trial judge unless appeal involves question of law only) substitute—

"(2) An appeal under this section lies only—

(a) with the leave of the Court; or

(b) if the judge of the court of trial grants a certificate that the case is fit for appeal."

Grounds for allowing and dismissing appeals.

2.—(1) In section 2 of the 1968 Act (disposal of appeal against conviction), for subsection (1) (grounds on which Court of Appeal are to allow or dismiss appeal), including the proviso, substitute—

"(1) Subject to the provisions of this Act, the Court of Appeal—

(a) shall allow an appeal against conviction if they think that the conviction is unsafe; and

(b) shall dismiss such an appeal in any other case."

(2) In section 2 of the 1980 Act (disposal of appeal against conviction), for subsection (1) (grounds on which Court of Appeal is to allow or dismiss appeal), including the proviso, substitute—

"(1) Subject to the provisions of this Act, the Court of Appeal—

(a) shall allow an appeal against conviction if it thinks that the conviction is unsafe; and

(b) shall dismiss such an appeal in any other case."

(3) In section 13 of the 1968 Act (disposal of appeal against verdict of not guilty by reason of insanity), for subsections (1) and (2) (grounds on which Court of Appeal are to allow or dismiss appeal) substitute—

"(1) Subject to the provisions of this section, the Court of Appeal—

(a) shall allow an appeal under section 12 of this Act if they think that the verdict is unsafe; and

(b) shall dismiss such an appeal in any other case."

(4) In section 12 of the 1980 Act (appeal against finding of not guilty on ground of insanity), for subsections (2) and (3) (grounds on which Court of Appeal is to allow or dismiss appeal) substitute—

"(2) Subject to subsection (4) below, the Court—

(a) shall allow an appeal under this section if it thinks that the finding is unsafe; and

(b) shall dismiss such an appeal in any other case."

(5) In section 16 of the 1968 Act (disposal of appeal against finding of disability), for subsection (1) (grounds on which Court of Appeal are to allow or dismiss appeal) substitute—

"(1) The Court of Appeal—

(a) shall allow an appeal under section 15 of this Act against a finding if they think that the finding is unsafe; and

(b) shall dismiss such an appeal in any other case."

(6) In section 13A of the 1980 Act (appeal against finding of unfitness to be tried), for subsections (3) and (4) (grounds on which Court of Appeal is to allow or dismiss appeal) substitute—

"(3) The Court—

(a) shall allow an appeal under this section if it thinks that the finding is unsafe; and

(b) shall dismiss such an appeal in any other case (except one to which subsection (5) below applies)."

Abolition of references by Secretary of State.

3. Section 17 of the 1968 Act and section 14 of the 1980 Act (which provide for references by Secretary of State to Court of Appeal of cases tried on indictment) shall cease to have effect.

Evidence.

4.—(1) In section 23 of the 1968 Act (evidence)—

(a) in subsection (1) (power to receive evidence etc.), for paragraph (c) substitute—

"(c) receive any evidence which was not adduced in the proceedings from which the appeal lies.",

(b) for subsection (2) (duty to receive evidence in certain circumstances) substitute—

"(2) The Court of Appeal shall, in considering whether to receive any evidence, have regard in particular to—

(a) whether the evidence appears to the Court to be capable of belief;

(b) whether it appears to the Court that the evidence may afford any ground for allowing the appeal;

(c) whether the evidence would have been admissible in the proceedings from which the appeal lies on an issue which is the subject of the appeal; and

(d) whether there is a reasonable explanation for the failure to adduce the evidence in those proceedings.", and

(c) in subsection (3), after "any" insert "evidence of a".

(2) In section 25 of the 1980 Act (evidence)—

(a) in subsection (1) (power to receive evidence etc.), for paragraph (c) substitute—

"(c) receive any evidence which was not adduced at the trial.",

(b) for subsection (2) (duty to receive evidence in certain circumstances) substitute—

"(2) The Court of Appeal shall, in considering whether to receive any evidence, have regard in particular to—

(a) whether the evidence appears to the Court to be capable of belief;

(b) whether it appears to the Court that the evidence may afford any ground for allowing the appeal;

(c) whether the evidence would have been admissible at the trial on an issue which is the subject of the appeal; and

(d) whether there is a reasonable explanation for the failure to adduce the evidence at the trial.", and

(c) in subsection (3), after "any" insert "evidence of a".

5.—(1) After section 23 of the 1968 Act insert— Power to order investigations.

"Power to order investigations.

23A.—(1) On an appeal against conviction the Court of Appeal may direct the Criminal Cases Review Commission to investigate and report to the Court on any matter if it appears to the Court that—

(a) the matter is relevant to the determination of the case and ought, if possible, to be resolved before the case is determined;

(b) an investigation of the matter by the Commission is likely to result in the Court being able to resolve it; and

(c) the matter cannot be resolved by the Court without an investigation by the Commission.

(2) A direction by the Court of Appeal under

subsection (1) above shall be given in writing and shall specify the matter to be investigated.

(3) Copies of such a direction shall be made available to the appellant and the respondent.

(4) Where the Commission have reported to the Court of Appeal on any matter which they have been directed under subsection (1) above to investigate, the Court—

(a) shall notify the appellant and the respondent that the Commission have reported; and

(b) may make available to the appellant and the respondent the report of the Commission and any statements, opinions and reports which accompanied it."

(2) After section 25 of the 1980 Act insert—

"Power to order investigations.

25A.—(1) On an appeal against conviction the Court of Appeal may direct the Criminal Cases Review Commission to investigate and report to the Court on any matter if it appears to the Court that—

(a) the matter is relevant to the determination of the case and ought, if possible, to be resolved before the case is determined;

(b) an investigation of the matter by the Commission is likely to result in the Court being able to resolve it; and

(c) the matter cannot be resolved by the Court without an investigation by the Commission.

(2) A direction by the Court under subsection (1) above shall be given in writing and shall specify the matter to be investigated.

(3) Copies of such a direction shall be made available to the appellant and the respondent.

(4) Where the Commission have reported to the Court of Appeal on any matter which they have

been directed under subsection (1) above to investigate, the Court—

(a) shall notify the appellant and the respondent that the Commission have reported; and

(b) may make available to the appellant and the respondent the report of the Commission and any statements, opinions and reports which accompanied it."

6. After section 31 of the 1968 Act insert— Powers exercisable by registrar.

"Powers of Court under Part I which are exercisable by registrar.

31A.—(1) The powers of the Court of Appeal under this Part of this Act which are specified in subsection (2) below may be exercised by the registrar.

(2) The powers mentioned in subsection (1) above are the following—

(a) to extend the time within which notice of appeal or of application for leave to appeal may be given;

(b) to order a witness to attend for examination; and

(c) to vary the conditions of bail granted to an appellant by the Court of Appeal or the Crown Court.

(3) No variation of the conditions of bail granted to an appellant may be made by the registrar unless he is satisfied that the respondent does not object to the variation; but, subject to that, the powers specified in that subsection are to be exercised by the registrar in the same manner as by the Court of Appeal and subject to the same provisions.

(4) If the registrar refuses an application on the part of an appellant to exercise in his favour any of the powers specified in subsection (2) above, the appellant shall be entitled to have the application determined by a single judge."

Appeals in cases of death.

7.—(1) Immediately before section 45 of the 1968 Act insert—

"Appeals in cases of death.

44A.—(1) Where a person has died—

(a) any relevant appeal which might have been begun by him had he remained alive may be begun by a person approved by the Court of Appeal; and

(b) where any relevant appeal was begun by him while he was alive or is begun in relation to his case by virtue of paragraph (a) above or by a reference by the Criminal Cases Review Commission, any further step which might have been taken by him in connection with the appeal if he were alive may be taken by a person so approved.

(2) In this section "relevant appeal" means—

(a) an appeal under section 1, 9, 12 or 15 of this Act; or

(b) an appeal under section 33 of this Act from any decision of the Court of Appeal on an appeal under any of those sections.

(3) Approval for the purposes of this section may only be given to—

(a) the widow or widower of the dead person;

(b) a person who is the personal representative (within the meaning of section 55(1)(xi) of the Administration of Estates Act 1925) of the dead person; or

1925 c. 23.

(c) any other person appearing to the Court of Appeal to have, by reason of a family or similar relationship with the dead person, a substantial financial or other interest in the determination of a relevant appeal relating to him.

(4) Except in the case of an appeal begun by a reference by the Criminal Cases Review Commission, an application for such approval may not be

made after the end of the period of one year beginning with the date of death.

(5) Where this section applies, any reference in this Act to the appellant shall, where appropriate, be construed as being or including a reference to the person approved under this section.

(6) The power of the Court of Appeal to approve a person under this section may be exercised by a single judge in the same manner as by the Court of Appeal and subject to the same provisions; but if the single judge refuses the application, the applicant shall be entitled to have the application determined by the Court of Appeal."

(2) After section 47 of the 1980 Act insert—

"Appeals in cases of death.

47A.—(1) Where a person has died—

(a) any relevant appeal which might have been begun by him had he remained alive may be begun by a person approved by the Court of Appeal; and

(b) where any relevant appeal was begun by him while he was alive or is begun in relation to his case by virtue of paragraph (a) above or by a reference by the Criminal Cases Review Commission, any further step which might have been taken by him in connection with the appeal if he were alive may be taken by a person so approved.

(2) In this section "relevant appeal" means—

(a) an appeal under section 1, 8, 9, 12 or 13A of this Act; or

(b) an appeal under section 31 of this Act from any decision of the Court of Appeal on an appeal under any of those sections.

(3) Approval for the purposes of this section may only be given to—

(a) the widow or widower of the dead person;

S.I. 1994/1899 (N.I.13).

(b) a person who is the personal representative (within the meaning of the Wills and Administration Proceedings (Northern Ireland) Order 1994) of the dead person; or

(c) any other person appearing to the Court of Appeal to have, by reason of a family or similar relationship with the dead person, a substantial financial or other interest in the determination of a relevant appeal relating to him.

(4) Except in the case of an appeal begun by a reference by the Criminal Cases Review Commission, an application for such approval may not be made after the end of the period of one year beginning with the date of death.

(5) Where this section applies, any reference in this Act to the appellant shall, where appropriate, be construed as being or including a reference to the person approved under this section."

PART II

THE CRIMINAL CASES REVIEW COMMISSION

The Commission

The Commission.

8.—(1) There shall be a body corporate to be known as the Criminal Cases Review Commission.

(2) The Commission shall not be regarded as the servant or agent of the Crown or as enjoying any status, immunity or privilege of the Crown; and the Commission's property shall not be regarded as property of, or held on behalf of, the Crown.

(3) The Commission shall consist of not fewer than eleven members.

(4) The members of the Commission shall be appointed by Her Majesty on the recommendation of the Prime Minister.

(5) At least one third of the members of the Commission shall be persons who are legally qualified; and for this purpose a person is legally qualified if—

(a) he has a ten year general qualification, within the meaning of section 71 of the Courts and Legal Services Act 1990, or 1990 c. 41.

(b) he is a member of the Bar of Northern Ireland, or solicitor of the Supreme Court of Northern Ireland, of at least ten years' standing.

(6) At least two thirds of the members of the Commission shall be persons who appear to the Prime Minister to have knowledge or experience of any aspect of the criminal justice system and of them at least one shall be a person who appears to him to have knowledge or experience of any aspect of the criminal justice system in Northern Ireland; and for the purposes of this subsection the criminal justice system includes, in particular, the investigation of offences and the treatment of offenders.

(7) Schedule 1 (further provisions with respect to the Commission) shall have effect.

References to court

Cases dealt with on indictment in England and Wales.

9.—(1) Where a person has been convicted of an offence on indictment in England and Wales, the Commission—

(a) may at any time refer the conviction to the Court of Appeal, and

(b) (whether or not they refer the conviction) may at any time refer to the Court of Appeal any sentence (not being a sentence fixed by law) imposed on, or in subsequent proceedings relating to, the conviction.

(2) A reference under subsection (1) of a person's conviction shall be treated for all purposes as an appeal by the person under section 1 of the 1968 Act against the conviction.

(3) A reference under subsection (1) of a sentence imposed on, or in subsequent proceedings relating to, a person's conviction on an indictment shall be treated for all purposes as an appeal by the person under section 9 of the 1968 Act against—

(a) the sentence, and

(b) any other sentence (not being a sentence fixed by law) imposed on, or in subsequent proceedings relating to, the conviction or any other conviction on the indictment.

(4) On a reference under subsection (1) of a person's conviction on an indictment the Commission may give notice to the Court of Appeal that any other conviction on the indictment which is specified in the notice is to be treated as referred to the Court of Appeal under subsection (1).

(5) Where a verdict of not guilty by reason of insanity has been returned in England and Wales in the case of a person, the Commission may at any time refer the verdict to the Court of Appeal; and a reference under this subsection shall be treated for all purposes as an appeal by the person under section 12 of the 1968 Act against the verdict.

(6) Where a jury in England and Wales has returned findings that a person is under a disability and that he did the act or made the omission charged against him, the Commission may at any time refer either or both of those findings to the Court of Appeal; and a reference under this subsection shall be treated for all purposes as an appeal by the person under section 15 of the 1968 Act against the finding or findings referred.

Cases dealt with on indictment in Northern Ireland.

10.—(1) Where a person has been convicted of an offence on indictment in Northern Ireland, the Commission—

(a) may at any time refer the conviction to the Court of Appeal, and

(b) (whether or not they refer the conviction) may at any time refer to the Court of Appeal any sentence (not being a sentence fixed by law) imposed on, or in subsequent proceedings relating to, the conviction.

(2) A reference under subsection (1) of a person's conviction shall be treated for all purposes as an appeal by the person under section 1 of the 1980 Act against the conviction.

(3) A reference under subsection (1) of a sentence imposed on, or in subsequent proceedings relating to, a person's conviction on an indictment shall be treated for all purposes as an appeal by the

person under section 8 or 9 (as the case may be) of the 1980 Act against—

(a) the sentence, and

(b) any other sentence (not being a sentence fixed by law) imposed on, or in subsequent proceedings relating to, the conviction or any other conviction on the indictment.

(4) On a reference under subsection (1) of a person's conviction on an indictment the Commission may give notice to the Court of Appeal that any other conviction on the indictment which is specified in the notice is to be treated as referred to the Court of Appeal under subsection (1).

(5) On a reference under subsection (1) the Court of Appeal may not pass any sentence more severe than that passed by the Crown Court.

(6) Where a finding of not guilty on the ground of insanity has been recorded in Northern Ireland in the case of a person, the Commission may at any time refer the finding to the Court of Appeal; and a reference under this subsection shall be treated for all purposes as an appeal by the person under section 12 of the 1980 Act against the finding.

(7) Where a jury in Northern Ireland has returned a finding that a person is unfit to be tried, the Commission may at any time refer the finding to the Court of Appeal; and a reference under this subsection shall be treated for all purposes as an appeal by the person under section 13A of the 1980 Act against the finding.

Cases dealt with summarily in England and Wales.

11.—(1) Where a person has been convicted of an offence by a magistrates' court in England and Wales, the Commission—

(a) may at any time refer the conviction to the Crown Court, and

(b) (whether or not they refer the conviction) may at any time refer to the Crown Court any sentence imposed on, or in subsequent proceedings relating to, the conviction.

(2) A reference under subsection (1) of a person's conviction shall be treated for all purposes as an appeal by the person under

1980 c. 43.

section 108(1) of the Magistrates' Courts Act 1980 against the conviction (whether or not he pleaded guilty).

(3) A reference under subsection (1) of a sentence imposed on, or in subsequent proceedings relating to, a person's conviction shall be treated for all purposes as an appeal by the person under section 108(1) of the Magistrates' Courts Act 1980 against—

(a) the sentence, and

(b) any other sentence imposed on, or in subsequent proceedings relating to, the conviction or any related conviction.

(4) On a reference under subsection (1) of a person's conviction the Commission may give notice to the Crown Court that any related conviction which is specified in the notice is to be treated as referred to the Crown Court under subsection (1).

(5) For the purposes of this section convictions are related if they are convictions of the same person by the same court on the same day.

(6) On a reference under this section the Crown Court may not award any punishment more severe than that awarded by the court whose decision is referred.

(7) The Crown Court may grant bail to a person whose conviction or sentence has been referred under this section; and any time during which he is released on bail shall not count as part of any term of imprisonment or detention under his sentence.

Cases dealt with summarily in Northern Ireland.

12.—(1) Where a person has been convicted of an offence by a magistrates' court in Northern Ireland, the Commission—

(a) may at any time refer the conviction to a county court, and

(b) (whether or not they refer the conviction) may at any time refer to a county court any sentence imposed on, or in subsequent proceedings relating to, the conviction.

(2) A reference under subsection (1) of a person's conviction shall be treated for all purposes as an appeal by the person under Article 140(1) of the Magistrates' Courts (Northern Ireland) Order 1981 against the conviction (whether or not he pleaded guilty).

S.I. 1981/1675 (N.I.26).

(3) A reference under subsection (1) of a sentence imposed on, or in subsequent proceedings relating to, a person's conviction shall be treated for all purposes as an appeal by the person under Article 140(1) of the Magistrates' Courts (Northern Ireland) Order 1981 against—

(a) the sentence, and

(b) any other sentence imposed on, or in subsequent proceedings relating to, the conviction or any related conviction.

(4) On a reference under subsection (1) of a person's conviction the Commission may give notice to the county court that any related conviction which is specified in the notice is to be treated as referred to the county court under subsection (1).

(5) For the purposes of this section convictions are related if they are convictions of the same person by the same court on the same day.

(6) On a reference under this section a county court may not award any punishment more severe than that awarded by the court whose decision is referred.

(7) The High Court may grant bail to a person whose conviction or sentence has been referred to a county court under this section; and any time during which he is released on bail shall not count as part of any term of imprisonment or detention under his sentence.

Conditions for making of references.

13.—(1) A reference of a conviction, verdict, finding or sentence shall not be made under any of sections 9 to 12 unless—

(a) the Commission consider that there is a real possibility that the conviction, verdict, finding or sentence would not be upheld were the reference to be made,

(b) the Commission so consider—

(i) in the case of a conviction, verdict or finding, because of an argument, or evidence, not raised in the proceedings which led to it or on any appeal or application for leave to appeal against it, or

(ii) in the case of a sentence, because of an argument on a point of law, or information, not so raised, and

(c) an appeal against the conviction, verdict, finding or sentence has been determined or leave to appeal against it has been refused.

(2) Nothing in subsection (1)(b)(i) or (c) shall prevent the making of a reference if it appears to the Commission that there are exceptional circumstances which justify making it.

Further provisions about references.

14.—(1) A reference of a conviction, verdict, finding or sentence may be made under any of sections 9 to 12 either after an application has been made by or on behalf of the person to whom it relates or without an application having been so made.

(2) In considering whether to make a reference of a conviction, verdict, finding or sentence under any of sections 9 to 12 the Commission shall have regard to—

(a) any application or representations made to the Commission by or on behalf of the person to whom it relates,

(b) any other representations made to the Commission in relation to it, and

(c) any other matters which appear to the Commission to be relevant.

(3) In considering whether to make a reference under section 9 or 10 the Commission may at any time refer any point on which they desire the assistance of the Court of Appeal to that Court for the Court's opinion on it; and on a reference under this subsection the Court of Appeal shall consider the point referred and furnish the Commission with the Court's opinion on the point.

(4) Where the Commission make a reference under any of sections 9 to 12 the Commission shall—

(a) give to the court to which the reference is made a statement of the Commission's reasons for making the reference, and

(b) send a copy of the statement to every person who appears to the Commission to be likely to be a party to any proceedings on the appeal arising from the reference.

(5) Where a reference under any of sections 9 to 12 is treated as

an appeal against any conviction, verdict, finding or sentence, the appeal may be on any ground relating to the conviction, verdict, finding or sentence (whether or not the ground is related to any reason given by the Commission for making the reference).

(6) in every case in which—

(a) an application has been made to the Commission by or on behalf of any person for the reference under any of sections 9 to 12 of any conviction, verdict, finding or sentence, but

(b) the Commission decide not to make a reference of the conviction, verdict, finding or sentence,

the Commission shall give a statement of the reasons for their decision to the person who made the application.

Investigations and assistance

Investigations for Court of Appeal.

15.—(1) Where a direction is given by the Court of Appeal under section 23A(1) of the 1968 Act or section 25A(1) of the 1980 Act the Commission shall investigate the matter specified in the direction in such manner as the Commission think fit.

(2) Where, in investigating a matter specified in such a direction, it appears to the Commission that—

(a) another matter (a "related matter") which is relevant to the determination of the case by the Court of Appeal ought, if possible, to be resolved before the case is determined by that Court, and

(b) an investigation of the related matter is likely to result in the Court's being able to resolve it,

the Commission may also investigate the related matter.

(3) The Commission shall—

(a) keep the Court of Appeal informed as to the progress of the investigation of any matter specified in a direction under section 23A(1) of the 1968 Act or section 25A(1) of the 1980 Act, and

(b) if they decide to investigate any related matter, notify the

Court of Appeal of their decision and keep the Court informed as to the progress of the investigation.

(4) The Commission shall report to the Court of Appeal on the investigation of any matter specified in a direction under section 23A(1) of the 1968 Act or section 25A(1) of the 1980 Act when—

(a) they complete the investigation of that matter and of any related matter investigated by them, or

(b) they are directed to do so by the Court of Appeal,

whichever happens first.

(5) A report under subsection (4) shall include details of any inquiries made by or for the Commission in the investigation of the matter specified in the direction or any related matter investigated by them.

(6) Such a report shall be accompanied—

(a) by any statements and opinions received by the Commission in the investigation of the matter specified in the direction or any related matter investigated by them, and

(b) subject to subsection (7), by any reports so received.

(7) Such a report need not be accompanied by any reports submitted to the Commission under section 20(6) by an investigating officer.

Assistance in connection with prerogative of mercy.

16.—(1) Where the Secretary of State refers to the Commission any matter which arises in the consideration of whether to recommend the exercise of Her Majesty's prerogative of mercy in relation to a conviction and on which he desires their assistance, the Commission shall—

(a) consider the matter referred, and

(b) give to the Secretary of State a statement of their conclusions on it;

and the Secretary of State shall, in considering whether so to recommend, treat the Commission's statement as conclusive of the matter referred.

(2) Where in any case the Commission are of the opinion that the Secretary of State should consider whether to recommend the exercise of Her Majesty's prerogative of mercy in relation to the case they shall give him the reasons for their opinion.

Supplementary powers

17.—(1) This section applies where the Commission believe that a person serving in a public body has possession or control of a document or other material which may assist the Commission in the exercise of any of their functions.

Power to obtain documents etc.

(2) Where it is reasonable to do so, the Commission may require the person who is the appropriate person in relation to the public body—

(a) to produce the document or other material to the Commission or to give the Commission access to it, and

(b) to allow the Commission to take away the document or other material or to make and take away a copy of it in such form as they think appropriate,

and may direct that person that the document or other material must not be destroyed, damaged or altered before the direction is withdrawn by the Commission.

(3) The documents and other material covered by this section include, in particular, any document or other material obtained or created during any investigation or proceedings relating to—

(a) the case in relation to which the Commission's function is being or may be exercised, or

(b) any other case which may be in any way connected with that case (whether or not any function of the Commission could be exercised in relation to that other case).

(4) The duty to comply with a requirement under this section is not affected by any obligation of secrecy or other limitation on disclosure (including any such obligation or limitation imposed by or by virtue of an enactment) which would otherwise prevent the production of the document or other material to the Commission or the giving of access to it to the Commission.

Government documents etc. relating to current or old cases.

18.—(1) Section 17 does not apply to any document or other material in the possession or control of a person serving in a government department if the document or other material—

(a) is relevant to a case to which this subsection applies, and

(b) is in the possession or control of the person in consequence of the Secretary of State's consideration of the case.

(2) Subsection (1) applies to a case if the Secretary of State—

(a) is, immediately before the day on which the repeal by this Act of section 17 of the 1968 Act or of section 14 of the 1980 Act comes into force, considering the case with a view to deciding whether to make a reference under that section or whether to recommend the exercise of Her Majesty's prerogative of mercy in relation to a conviction by a magistrates' court, or

(b) has at any earlier time considered the case with a view to deciding whether to make such a reference or whether so to recommend.

(3) The Secretary of State shall give to the Commission any document or other material which—

(a) contains representations made to him in relation to any case to which this subsection applies, or

(b) was received by him in connection with any such case otherwise than from a person serving in a government department,

and may give to the Commission any document or other material which is relevant to any such case but does not fall within paragraph (a) or (b).

(4) Subsection (3) applies to a case if—

(a) the Secretary of State is, immediately before the day on which the repeal by this Act of section 17 of the 1968 Act or of section 14 of the 1980 Act comes into force, considering the case with a view to deciding whether to make a reference under that section or whether to recommend the exercise of Her Majesty's prerogative of mercy in relation to a conviction by a magistrates' court, or

(b) the Secretary of State has at any earlier time considered the case with a view to deciding whether to make such a reference, or whether so to recommend, and the Commission at any time notify him that they wish subsection (3) to apply to the case.

19.—(1) Where the Commission believe that inquiries should be made for assisting them in the exercise of any of their functions in relation to any case they may require the appointment of an investigating officer to carry out the inquiries.

Power to require appointment of investigating officers.

(2) Where any offence to which the case relates was investigated by persons serving in a public body, a requirement under this section may be imposed—

(a) on the person who is the appropriate person in relation to the public body, or

(b) where the public body has ceased to exist, on any chief officer of police or on the person who is the appropriate person in relation to any public body which appears to the Commission to have functions which consist of or include functions similar to any of those of the public body which has ceased to exist.

(3) Where no offence to which the case relates was investigated by persons serving in a public body, a requirement under this section may be imposed on any chief officer of police.

(4) A requirement under this section imposed on a chief officer of police may be—

(a) a requirement to appoint a person serving in the police force in relation to which he is the chief officer of police, or

(b) a requirement to appoint a person serving in another police force selected by the chief officer.

(5) A requirement under this section imposed on a person who is the appropriate person in relation to a public body other than a police force may be—

(a) A requirement to appoint a person serving in the public body, or

(b) a requirement to appoint a person serving in a police force, or in a public body (other than a police force) having functions which consist of or include the investigation of offences, selected by the appropriate person.

(6) The Commission may direct—

(a) that a person shall not be appointed, or

(b) that a police force or other public body shall not be selected,

under subsection (4) or (5) without the approval of the Commission.

(7) Where an appointment is made under this section by the person who is the appropriate person in relation to any public body, that person shall inform the Commission of the appointment; and if the Commission are not satisfied with the person appointed they may direct that—

(a) the person who is the appropriate person in relation to the public body shall, as soon as is reasonably practicable, select another person in his place and notify the Commission of the proposal to appoint the other person, and

(b) the other person shall not be appointed without the approval of the Commission.

Inquiries by investigating officers.

20.—(1) A person appointed as the investigating officer in relation to a case shall undertake such inquiries as the Commission may from time to time reasonably direct him to undertake in relation to the case.

(2) A person appointed as an investigating officer shall be permitted to act as such by the person who is the appropriate person in relation to the public body in which he is serving.

(3) Where the chief officer of an England and Wales police force appoints a member of the Royal Ulster Constabulary as an investigating officer, the member appointed shall have in England and Wales the same powers and privileges as a member of the police force has there as a constable; and where the Chief Constable of the Royal Ulster Constabulary appoints a member of an England and Wales police force as an investigating officer, the member appointed shall have in Northern Ireland the same powers

and privileges as a member of the Royal Ulster Constabulary has there as a constable.

(4) The Commission may take any steps which they consider appropriate for supervising the undertaking of inquiries by an investigating officer.

(5) The Commission may at any time direct that a person appointed as the investigating officer in relation to a case shall cease to act as such; but the making of such a direction shall not prevent the Commission from imposing a requirement under section 19 to appoint another investigating officer in relation to the case.

(6) When a person appointed as the investigating officer in relation to a case has completed the inquiries which he has been directed by the Commission to undertake in relation to the case, he shall—

(a) prepare a report of his findings,

(b) submit it to the Commission, and

(c) send a copy of it to the person by whom he was appointed.

(7) When a person appointed as the investigating officer in relation to a case submits to the Commission a report of his findings he shall also submit to them any statements, opinions and reports received by him in connection with the inquiries which he was directed to undertake in relation to the case.

Other powers.

21. Sections 17 to 20 are without prejudice to the taking by the Commission of any steps which they consider appropriate for assisting them in the exercise of any of their functions including, in particular—

(a) undertaking, or arranging for others to undertake, inquiries, and

(b) obtaining, or arranging for others to obtain, statements, opinions and reports.

Meaning of "public body" etc.

22.—(1) In sections 17, 19 and 20 and this section "public body" means—

(a) any police force,

(b) any government department, local authority or other body constituted for purposes of the public service, local government or the administration of justice, or

(c) any other body whose members are appointed by Her Majesty, any Minister or any government department or whose revenues consist wholly or mainly of money provided by Parliament or appropriated by Measure of the Northern Ireland Assembly.

(2) In sections 19 and 20 and this section—

(a) "police force" includes the Royal Ulster Constabulary and the Royal Ulster Constabulary Reserve and any body of constables maintained otherwise than by a police authority,

(b) references to the chief officer of police, in relation to the Royal Ulster Constabulary and the Royal Ulster Constabulary Reserve, are to the Chief Constable of the Constabulary and, in relation to a police force maintained otherwise than by a police authority, are to the chief constable, and

(c) references to an England and Wales police force are to a police force maintained under section 2 of the Police Act 1964, the metropolitan police force or the City of London police force.

1964 c. 48.

(3) In section 18 and this section—

(a) references to a government department include a Northern Ireland department and the Office of the Director of Public Prosecutions for Northern Ireland, and

(b) "Minister" means a Minister of the Crown as defined by section 8 of the Ministers of the Crown Act 1975 but also includes the head of a Northern Ireland department.

1975 c. 26.

(4) In sections 17, 19 and 20 "the appropriate person" means—

(a) in relation to a police force, the chief officer of police,

(b) in relation to the Crown Prosecution Service, the Director of Public Prosecutions,

(c) in relation to the Office of the Director of Public Prosecutions for Northern Ireland, that Director,

(d) in relation to the Serious Fraud Office, the Director of the Serious Fraud Office,

(e) in relation to the Inland Revenue, the Commissioners of Inland Revenue,

(f) in relation to the Customs and Excise, the Commissioners of Customs and Excise,

(g) in relation to any government department not within any of the preceding paragraphs, the Minister in charge of the department, and

(h) in relation to any public body not within any of the preceding paragraphs, the public body itself (if it is a body corporate) or the person in charge of the public body (if it is not).

(5) For the purposes of sections 17, 19 and 20—

(a) a justices' chief executive or justices' clerk appointed by, or a member of the staff of, a magistrates' courts committee shall be treated as serving in the committee, and

(b) a person authorised under section 57 of the Northern Ireland (Emergency Provisions) Act 1991 to exercise the powers conferred by Schedule 5 to that Act shall be treated as if he were serving in a public body and he were the appropriate person in relation to the body. 1991 c. 24.

Disclosure of information

23.—(1) A person who is or has been a member or employee of the Commission shall not disclose any information obtained by the Commission in the exercise of any of their functions unless the disclosure of the information is excepted from this section by section 24. Offence of disclosure.

(2) A person who is or has been an investigating officer shall not disclose any information obtained by him in his inquiries unless the disclosure of the information is excepted from this section by section 24.

(3) A member of the Commission shall not authorise—

(a) the disclosure by an employee of the Commission of any information obtained by the Commission in the exercise of any of their functions, or

(b) the disclosure by an investigating officer of any information obtained by him in his inquiries,

unless the authorisation of the disclosure of the information is excepted from this section by section 24.

(4) A person who contravenes this section is guilty of an offence and liable on summary conviction to a fine of an amount not exceeding level 5 on the standard scale.

Exceptions from obligations of non-disclosure.

24.—(1) The disclosure of information, or the authorisation of the disclosure of information, is excepted from section 23 by this section if the information is disclosed, or is authorised to be disclosed—

(a) for the purposes of any criminal, disciplinary or civil proceedings,

(b) in order to assist in dealing with an application made to the Secretary of State for compensation for a miscarriage of justice,

(c) by a person who is a member or an employee of the Commission either to another person who is a member or an employee of the Commission or to an investigating officer,

(d) by an investigating officer to a member or an employee of the Commission,

(e) in any statement or report required by this Act,

(f) in or in connection with the exercise of any function under this Act, or

(g) in any circumstances in which the disclosure of information is permitted by an order made by the Secretary of State.

(2) The disclosure of information is also excepted from section 23 by this section if the information is disclosed by an employee of the Commission, or an investigating officer, who is authorised to disclose the information by a member of the Commission.

(3) The disclosure of information, or the authorisation of the disclosure of information, is also excepted from section 23 by this section if the information is disclosed, or is authorised to be disclosed, for the purposes of—

(a) the investigation of an offence, or

(b) deciding whether to prosecute a person for an offence,

unless the disclosure is or would be prevented by an obligation of secrecy or other limitation on disclosure (including any such obligation or limitation imposed by or by virtue of an enactment) arising otherwise than under that section.

(4) Where the disclosure of information is excepted from section 23 by subsection (1) or (2), the disclosure of the information is not prevented by any obligation of secrecy or other limitation on disclosure (including any such obligation or limitation imposed by or by virtue of an enactment) arising otherwise than under that section.

(5) The power to make an order under subsection (1)(g) is exercisable by statutory instrument which shall be subject to annulment in pursuance of a resolution of either House of Parliament.

Consent to disclosure.

25.—(1) Where a person on whom a requirement is imposed under section 17 notifies the Commission that any information contained in any document or other material to which the requirement relates is not to be disclosed by the Commission without his prior consent, the Commission shall not disclose the information without such consent.

(2) Such consent may not be withheld unless—

(a) (apart from section 17) the person would have been prevented by any obligation of secrecy or other limitation on disclosure from disclosing the information to the Commission, and

(b) it is reasonable for the person to withhold his consent to disclosure of the information by the Commission.

(3) An obligation of secrecy or other limitation on disclosure which applies to a person only where disclosure is not authorised by another person shall not be taken for the purposes of subsection

(2)(a) to prevent the disclosure by the person of information to the Commission unless—

(a) reasonable steps have been taken to obtain the authorisation of the other person, or

(b) such authorisation could not reasonably be expected to be obtained.

PART III

OTHER PROVISIONS

Powers of magistrates' courts to rectify mistakes

Extension of power of courts in England and Wales.

26.—(1) Section 142 of the Magistrates' Courts Act 1980 (power of magistrates' courts to re-open cases to rectify mistakes etc.) shall be amended as follows.

1980 c. 43.

(2) In subsection (1) (power, subject to subsection (4), to vary or rescind a sentence or other order), for the words from the beginning to "offender;" substitute "A magistrates' court may vary or rescind a sentence or other order imposed or made by it when dealing with an offender if it appears to the court to be in the interests of justice to do so;".

(3) After that subsection insert—

"(1A) The power conferred on a magistrates' court by subsection (1) above shall not be exercisable in relation to any sentence or order imposed or made by it when dealing with an offender if—

(a) the Crown Court has determined an appeal against—

(i) that sentence or order;

(ii) the conviction in respect of which that sentence or order was imposed or made; or

(iii) any other sentence or order imposed or made by the magistrates' court when dealing with the offender in respect of that conviction (including a sentence or order replaced by that sentence or order); or

(b) the High Court has determined a case stated for the opinion of that court on any question arising in any proceeding leading to or resulting from the imposition or making of the sentence or order."

(4) In subsection (2) (power, subject to subsection (4), to direct that a person's case be re-heard by different justices where he pleaded not guilty or the court proceeded in his absence)—

(a) for the words from "found guilty" to "section 11(1) above," substitute "convicted by a magistrates' court", and

(b) omit ", subject to subsection (4) below,".

(5) After that subsection insert—

"(2A) The power conferred on a magistrates' court by subsection (2) above shall not be exercisable in relation to a conviction if—

(a) the Crown Court has determined an appeal against—

(i) the conviction; or

(ii) any sentence or order imposed or made by the magistrates' court when dealing with the offender in respect of the conviction; or

(b) the High Court has determined a case stated for the opinion of that court on any question arising in any proceeding leading to or resulting from the conviction."

(6) In subsection (3) (effect of directions under subsection (2)), for "finding of guilty" substitute "conviction".

(7) Omit subsection (4) (powers in subsections (1) and (2) to be exercisable only within 28 days of making of sentence or order or finding of guilty and only by a similarly constituted court).

27. After Article 158 of the Magistrates' Courts (Northern Ireland) Order 1981 insert— Introduction of power in Northern Ireland.

"Power to rectify mistakes etc. S.I. 1981/1675 (N.I.26).

Power of magistrates' court to re-open cases to rectify mistakes etc.

158A.—(1) A magistrates' court may vary or rescind a

sentence or other order imposed or made by it when dealing with an offender if it appears to the court to be in the interests of justice to do so; and it is hereby declared that this power extends to replacing a sentence or order which for any reason appears to be invalid by another which the court has power to impose or make.

(2) The power conferred on a magistrates' court by paragraph (1) shall not be exercisable in relation to any sentence or order imposed or made by it when dealing with an offender if—

(a) the county court has determined an appeal against—

(i) that sentence or order;

(ii) the conviction in respect of which that sentence or order was imposed or made; or

(iii) any other sentence or order imposed or made by the magistrates' court when dealing with the offender in respect of that conviction (including a sentence or order replaced by that sentence or order); or

(b) the Court of Appeal has determined a case stated for the opinion of that court on any question arising in any proceeding leading to or resulting from the imposition or making of the sentence or order.

(3) Where a person is convicted by a magistrates' court and it subsequently appears to the court that it would be in the interests of justice that the case should be heard again by another resident magistrate or another justice of the peace (as the case may be), the court may so direct.

(4) The power conferred on a magistrates' court by paragraph (3) shall not be exercisable in relation to a conviction if—

(a) the county court has determined an appeal against—

(i) the conviction; or

(ii) any sentence or order imposed or made by

the magistrates' court when dealing with the offender in respect of the conviction; or

(b) the Court of Appeal has determined a case stated for the opinion of that court on any question arising in any proceeding leading to or resulting from the conviction.

(5) Where a court gives a direction under paragraph (3)—

(a) the conviction and any sentence or other order imposed or made in consequence of it shall be of no effect; and

(b) Article 47 shall apply as if the trial of the person in question had been adjourned.

(6) Where a sentence or order is varied under paragraph (1), the sentence or other order, as so varied, shall take effect from the beginning of the day on which it was originally imposed or made, unless the court otherwise directs."

Compensation for miscarriages of justice

28. In section 133 of the Criminal Justice Act 1988 (compensation for miscarriages of justice), after subsection (4) insert— Assessment of compensation.

"(4A) In assessing so much of any compensation payable under this section to or in respect of a person as is attributable to suffering, harm to reputation or similar damage, the assessor shall have regard in particular to— 1988 c. 33.

(a) the seriousness of the offence of which the person was convicted and the severity of the punishment resulting from the conviction;

(b) the conduct of the investigation and prosecution of the offence; and

(c) any other convictions of the person and any punishment resulting from them."

PART IV

SUPPLEMENTARY

Minor and consequential amendments and repeals.

29.—(1) Schedule 2 (minor and consequential amendments) shall have effect.

(2) The enactments specified in Schedule 3 (which include spent provisions) are repealed to the extent specified in the third column of that Schedule.

Interpretation.

30.—(1) In this Act—

1968 c. 19.

"the 1968 Act" means the Criminal Appeal Act 1968,

1980 c. 47.

"the 1980 Act" means the Criminal Appeal (Northern Ireland) Act 1980,

"the Commission" means the Criminal Cases Review Commission,

"enactment" includes an enactment comprised in Northern Ireland legislation, and

"investigating officer" means a person appointed under section 19 to carry out inquiries.

(2) In this Act "sentence"—

(a) in section 9 has the same meaning as in the 1968 Act,

(b) in section 10 has the same meaning as in Part I of the 1980 Act,

1980 c. 43.

(c) in section 11 has the same meaning as in section 108 of the Magistrates' Courts Act 1980, and

S.I. 1981/1675 (N.I.26).

(d) in section 12 has the same meaning as in Article 140(1) of the Magistrates' Courts (Northern Ireland) Order 1981.

Financial provision.

31.—(1) There shall be paid out of money provided by Parliament—

(a) any expenditure of the Secretary of State incurred in connection with the Commission, and

(b) any increase attributable to this Act in the sums payable under any other Act out of money so provided.

(2) Any sums received by the Treasury under or by virtue of this Act (so far as not used as an appropriation in aid) shall be paid into the Consolidated Fund.

32.—(1) This Act shall come into force on such day as the Secretary of State may by order made by statutory instrument appoint; and different days may be appointed for different provisions or for different purposes. Commencement.

(2) An order under subsection (1) may include such transitional provisions and savings as appear to the Secretary of State to be necessary or desirable.

33.—(1) The provisions of Parts I and III and of Schedules 2 and 3 have the same extent as the enactments which they amend or repeal. Extent.

(2) Section 8 and Schedule 1 and sections 13 to 25 extend only to England and Wales and Northern Ireland.

(3) Section 9 and 11 extend only to England and Wales.

(4) Sections 10 and 12 extend only to Northern Ireland.

34. This Act may be cited as the Criminal Appeal Act 1995. Short title.

SCHEDULES

Section 8.

SCHEDULE 1

THE COMMISSION: FURTHER PROVISIONS

Membership

1. Her Majesty shall, on the recommendation of the Prime Minister, appoint one of the members of the Commission to be the chairman of the Commission.

2.—(1) Subject to the following provisions of this paragraph, a person shall hold and vacate office as a member of the Commission, or as chairman of the Commission, in accordance with the terms of his appointment.

(2) An appointment as a member of the Commission may be full-time or part-time.

(3) The appointment of a person as a member of the Commission, or as chairman of the Commission, shall be for a fixed period of not longer than five years.

(4) Subject to sub-paragraph (5), a person whose term of appointment as a member of the Commission, or as chairman of the Commission, expires shall be eligible for re-appointment.

(5) No person may hold office as a member of the Commission for a continuous period which is longer than ten years.

(6) A person may at any time resign his office as a member of the Commission, or as chairman of the Commission, by notice in writing addressed to Her Majesty.

(7) Her Majesty may at any time remove a person from office as a member of the Commission if satisfied—

(a) that he has without reasonable excuse failed to discharge his functions as a member for a continuous period of three months beginning not earlier than six months before that time,

(b) that he has been convicted of a criminal offence,

(c) that a bankruptcy order has been made against him, or his estate has been sequestrated, or he has made a composition or arrangement with, or granted a trust deed for, his creditors, or

(d) that he is unable or unfit to discharge his functions as a member.

(8) If the chairman of the Commission ceases to be a member of the Commission he shall also cease to be chairman.

Members and employees

3.—(1) The Commission shall—

(a) pay to members of the Commission such remuneration,

(b) pay to or in respect of members of the Commission any such allowances, fees, expenses and gratuities, and

(c) pay towards the provision of pensions to or in respect of members of the Commission any such sums,

as the Commission are required to pay by or in accordance with directions given by the Secretary of State.

(2) Where a member of the Commission was, immediately before becoming a member, a participant in a scheme under section 1 of the Superannuation Act 1972, the Minister for the Civil Service may determine that his term of office as a member shall be treated for the purposes of the scheme as if it were service in the employment or office by reference to which he was a participant in the scheme; and his rights under the scheme shall not be affected by sub-paragraph (1)(c). 1972 c. 11.

(3) Where—

(a) a person ceases to hold office as a member of the Commission otherwise than on the expiry of his term of appointment, and

(b) it appears to the Secretary of State that there are special circumstances which make it right for him to receive compensation,

the Secretary of State may direct the Commission to make to him a payment of such amount as the Secretary of State may determine.

4.—(1) The Commission may appoint a chief executive and such other employees as the Commission think fit, subject to the consent of the Secretary of State as to their number and terms and conditions of service.

(2) The Commission shall—

(a) pay to employees of the Commission such remuneration, and

(b) pay to or in respect of employees of the Commission any such allowances, fees, expenses and gratuities, as the Commission may, with the consent of the Secretary of State, determine.

(3) Employment by the Commission shall be included among the kinds of employment to which a scheme under section 1 of the Superannuation Act 1972 may apply.

1972 c. 11.

5. The Commission shall pay to the Minister for the Civil Service, at such times as he may direct, such sums as he may determine in respect of any increase attributable to paragraph 3(2) or 4(3) in the sums payable out of money provided by Parliament under the Superannuation Act 1972.

Procedure

6.—(1) The arrangements for the procedure of the Commission (including the quorum for meetings) shall be such as the Commission may determine.

(2) The arrangements may provide for the discharge, under the general direction of the Commission, of any function of the Commission—

(a) in the case of a function specified in sub-paragraph (3), by a committee consisting of not fewer than three members of the Commission, and

(b) in any other case, by any committee of, or by one or more of the members or employees of, the Commission.

(3) The functions referred to in sub-paragraph (2)(a) are—

(a) making a reference to a court under any of sections 9 to 12,

(b) reporting to the Court of Appeal under section 15(4),

(c) giving to the Secretary of State a statement under section 16(1)(b), and

(d) requiring the appointment of an investigating officer under section 19.

(4) The validity of any proceedings of the Commission (or of any committee of the Commission) shall not be affected by—

(a) any vacancy among the members of the Commission or in the office of chairman of the Commission, or

(b) any defect in the appointment of any person as a member of the Commission or as chairman of the Commission.

(5) Where—

(a) a document or other material has been produced to the Commission under section 17, or they have been given access to a document or other material under that section, and the Commission have taken away the document or other material (or a copy of it), and

(b) the person who produced the document or other material to the Commission, or gave them access to it, has notified the Commission that he considers that its disclosure to others may be contrary to the interests of national security,

the Commission shall, after consulting that person, deal with the document or material (or copy) in a manner appropriate for safeguarding the interests of national security.

Evidence

7. A document purporting to be—

(a) duly executed under the seal of the Commission, or

(b) signed on behalf of the Commission,

shall be received in evidence and, unless the contrary is proved, taken to be so executed or signed.

Annual reports and accounts

8.—(1) As soon as possible after the end of each financial year of the Commission, the Commission shall send to the Secretary of State a report on the discharge of their functions during that year.

(2) Such a report may include an account of the working of the provisions of sections 9 to 25 and recommendations relating to any of those provisions.

(3) The Secretary of State shall lay before each House of Parliament, and cause to be published, a copy of every report sent to him under sub-paragraph (1).

9.—(1) The Commission shall—

(a) keep proper accounts and proper records in relation to the accounts, and

(b) prepare a statement of accounts in respect of each financial year of the Commission.

(2) The statement of accounts shall contain such information and shall be in such form as the Secretary of State may, with the consent of the Treasury, direct.

(3) The Commission shall send a copy of the statement of accounts to the Secretary of State and to the Comptroller and Auditor General within such period after the end of the financial year to which the statement relates as the Secretary of State may direct.

(4) The Comptroller and Auditor General shall—

(a) examine, certify and report on the statement of accounts, and

(b) lay a copy of the statement of accounts and of his report before each House of Parliament.

10. For the purposes of this Schedule the Commission's financial year shall be the period of twelve months ending with 31st March; but the first financial year of the Commission shall be the period beginning with the date of establishment of the Commission and ending with the first 31st March which falls at least six months after that date.

Expenses

11. The Secretary of State shall defray the expenses of the Commission up to such amount as may be approved by him.

Section 29.

SCHEDULE 2

MINOR AND CONSEQUENTIAL AMENDMENTS

The Army Act 1955 (c.18)

1. In section 110 of the Army Act 1955 (powers of confirming officers), for the words from "is under" in subsection (1) to the end of the proviso to that subsection substitute "is unsafe, or by confirming the finding or sentence or referring the finding or sentence (or both) for confirmation to a higher confirming officer."

The Air Force Act 1955 (c.19)

2. In section 110 of the Air Force Act 1955 (powers of confirming officers), for the words from "is under" in subsection (1) to the end of the

proviso to that subsection substitute "is unsafe, or by confirming the finding or sentence or referring the finding or sentence (or both) for confirmation to a higher confirming officer."

The Public Records Act 1958 (c.51)

3. In the First Schedule to the Public Records Act 1958 (definition of public records), in Part II of the Table at the end of paragraph 3, at the appropriate place insert—

"Criminal Cases Review Commission."

The Criminal Appeal Act 1968 (c.19)

4.—(1) The Criminal Appeal Act 1968 shall be amended as follows.

(2) In section 5 (disposal of appeal against conviction on special verdict), in subsection (1), for "by a person in whose case" substitute "in a case where".

(3) In section 23 (evidence), in subsections (1) and (4), for "purposes of" substitute "the purposes of an appeal under".

(4) In section 29 (effect of appeal on sentence), in subsection (2)(c), for "by the Secretary of State under section 17 of this Act" substitute "under section 9 of the Criminal Appeal Act 1995".

(5) In section 45 (construction of references to Court of Appeal and single judge)—

(a) in subsection (1) (references to Court of Appeal), after "II" insert "and section 44A", and

(b) in subsection (2) (references to single judge), for "and 44" substitute ", 31A, 44 and 44A".

The Courts-Martial (Appeals) Act 1968 (c.20)

5.—(1) The Courts-Martial (Appeals) Act 1968 shall be amended as follows.

(2) In section 12 (disposal of appeal against conviction by court-martial), for subsection (1) (grounds on which Courts-Martial Appeal Court are to allow or dismiss appeal), including the proviso, substitute—

"(1) The Appeal Court—

(a) shall allow an appeal against conviction by court-martial if they think that the conviction is unsafe; and

(b) shall dismiss such an appeal in any other case.",

and, in the side-note, for "wrong in law, etc" substitute "unsafe".

(3) In section 28 (evidence)—

(a) in subsection (1) (power to receive evidence etc.), for paragraph (c) substitute—

"(c) receive any evidence which was not adduced at the trial.",

(b) for subsection (2) (duty to receive evidence in certain circumstances) substitute—

"(2) The Appeal Court shall, in considering whether to receive any evidence, have regard in particular to—

(a) whether the evidence appears to the Court to be capable of belief;

(b) whether it appears to the Court that the evidence may afford any ground for allowing the appeal;

(c) whether the evidence would have been admissible at the trial on an issue which is the subject of the appeal; and

(d) whether there is a reasonable explanation for the failure to adduce the evidence at the trial.", and

(c) in subsection (3), after "any" insert "evidence of a".

The Costs in Criminal Cases Act (Northern Ireland) 1968 (c.10 (N.I.))

6. In section 4 of the Costs in Criminal Cases Act (Northern Ireland) 1968 (costs awarded by Court of Appeal), at the end insert—

"(5) Where section 47A of the Criminal Appeal (Northern Ireland) Act 1980 (death of convicted person) applies, any reference in this section to the appellant includes the person approved under that section."

The Superannuation Act 1972 (c.11)

7. In Schedule 1 to the Superannuation Act 1972 (kinds of employment to which a scheme under section 1 of that act may apply) at the end of the list of "Royal Commissions and other Commissions" insert—

"Criminal Cases Review Commission."

The Juries Act 1974 (c.23)

8. In Part I of Schedule 1 to the Juries Act 1974 (persons ineligible for jury service), in Group B, after the entry beginning "Members of the Parole Board" insert—

"Members and employees of the Criminal Cases Review Commission."

The Juries (Northern Ireland) Order 1974 (S.I.1974/2143 (N.I.6))

9. In Schedule 2 to the Juries (Northern Ireland) Order 1974 (exemptions from jury service), in the group headed "Persons concerned with administration of justice), at the end insert—

"Members and employees of the Criminal Cases Review Commission."

The House of Commons Disqualification Act 1975 (c.24)

10. In the House of Commons Disqualification Act 1975, in Part II of Schedule 1 (bodies of which all members are disqualified), at the appropriate place insert—

"the Criminal Cases Review Commission".

The Northern Ireland Assembly Disqualification Act 1975 (c.25)

11. In the Northern Ireland Assembly Disqualification Act 1975, in Part II of Schedule 1 (bodies of which all members are disqualified), at the appropriate place insert—

"the Criminal Cases Review Commission".

The Criminal Appeal (Northern Ireland) Act 1980 (c.47)

12.—(1) The Criminal Appeal (Northern Ireland) Act 1980 shall be amended as follows.

(2) In section 16 (notice of appeal or application for leave), in subsection (1), omit "appeal or".

(3) In section 25 (evidence), in subsection (1), after "purposes of" insert "an appeal under".

(4) In section 26 (additional powers of Court), in subsection (1), after "purposes of" insert "an appeal under".

(5) In section 29 (computation of sentence), in subsection (3)(c), for "section 14 of this Act" substitute "section 10 of the Criminal Appeal Act 1995".

(6) In section 45 (powers of the Court of Appeal exercisable by single judge), after subsection (3A) insert—

> "(3B) Subject to section 44(4) above, the power of the Court of Appeal to approve a person under section 47A of this Act may be exercised by a single judge of the Court."

The County Courts (Northern Ireland) Order 1980 (S.I.1980/397 (N.I.3))

13. In Article 28(3) of the County Courts (Northern Ireland) Order 1980 (power of county court to increase punishment on appeal), after "1954" insert "but subject to section 12(6) of the Criminal Appeal Act 1995".

The Supreme Court Act 1981 (c.54)

14. In section 48 of the Supreme Court Act 1981 (appeals to Crown Court), in subsection (4) (power to award more severe punishment), for "If" substitute "Subject to section 11(6) of the Criminal Appeal Act 1995, if".

The Prosecution Offences Act 1985 (c.23)

15. In section 21(1) of the Prosecution of Offences Act 1985 (interpretation of Part II), before the definition of "defendant's costs order" insert—

> " "accused" and "appellant", in a case where section 44A of the Criminal Appeal Act 1968 (death of convicted person) applies, include the person approved under that section;".

The Criminal Justice Act 1988 (c.33)

16.—(1) The Criminal Justice Act 1988 shall be amended as follows.

(2) In section 32 (evidence through television links), in subsection (1A) (proceedings where section applies)—

(a) in paragraph (a), for "section 17 of the Criminal Appeal Act 1968" substitute "section 9 of the Criminal Appeal Act 1995", and

(b) in paragraph (b), for "and appeals to the Crown Court arising out of such proceedings" substitute ", appeals to the Crown Court arising out of such proceedings and hearings of references under section 11 of the Criminal Appeal Act 1995 so arising".

(3) In section 32A (video recordings of testimony from child witnesses), in subsection (1) (proceedings where section applies)—

(a) in paragraph (b), for "section 17 of the Criminal Appeal Act 1968" substitute "section 9 of the Criminal Appeal Act 1995", and

(b) in paragraph (c), for "and appeals to the Crown Court arising out of such proceedings" substitute ", appeals to the Crown Court arising out of such proceedings and hearings of references under section 11 of the Criminal Appeal Act 1995 so arising".

(4) In section 133 (compensation for miscarriages of justice), in subsection (5) (meaning of "reversed" in relation to a conviction), in paragraph (b) (references), for sub-paragraph (i) substitute—

"(i) under the Criminal Appeal Act 1995; or",

and omit sub-paragraph (iii).

The Legal Aid Act 1988 (c.34)

17. In section 21 of the Legal Aid Act 1988 (availability of representation for the purposes of criminal proceedings), after subsection (10) insert—

"(10A) Where section 44A of the Criminal Appeal Act 1968 (death of convicted person) applies, the reference in subsection (1) above to the convicted person shall be construed as a reference to the person approved under that section."

The Police and Criminal Evidence (Northern Ireland) Order 1989 (S.I.1989/1341 (N.I.12))

18.—(1) The Police and Criminal Evidence (Northern Ireland) Order 1989 shall be amended as follows.

(2) In Article 81 (evidence through television links), in paragraph (1A) (proceedings where Article applies)—

(a) in sub-paragraph (a), for "section 14 of the Criminal Appeal (Northern Ireland) Act 1980" substitute "section 10 of the Criminal Appeal Act 1995", and

(b) in sub-paragraph (b), for "and appeals to the county court arising out of such proceedings" substitute ", appeals to the county court arising out of such proceedings and hearings of references under section 12 of the Criminal Appeal Act 1995 so arising".

(3) In Article 81A (video recordings of testimony from child witnesses), in paragraph (1) (proceedings where Article applies)—

(a) in sub-paragraph (b), for "section 14 of the Criminal Appeal (Northern Ireland) Act 1980" substitute "section 10 of the Criminal Appeal Act 1995", and

(b) in sub-paragraph (c), for "and appeals to the county court arising out of such proceedings" substitute ", appeals to the county court arising out of such proceedings and hearings of references under section 12 of the Criminal Appeal Act 1995 so arising".

The Criminal Justice and Public Order Act 1994 (c.33)

19. In section 51 of the Criminal Justice and Public Order Act 1994 (intimidation etc. of witnesses, jurors and others), in subsection (9), in the definition of "the relevant period", for "reference under section 17 of the Criminal Appeal Act 1968" substitute "a reference under section 9 or 11 of the Criminal Appeal Act 1995".

SCHEDULE 3

Section 29.

REPEALS

Chapter	Short title	Extent of repeal
1967 c. 13.	The Parliamentary Commissioner Act 1967.	In Schedule 3, in paragraph 7, the words "the Court of Appeal,".
1968 c. 19.	The Criminal Appeal Act 1968.	Section 17. In section 23(3), the words following "compellable".
1968 c. 20.	The Courts-Martial (Appeals) Act 1968.	In section 28(3), the words following "compellable".
1977 c. 45.	The Criminal Law Act 1977.	Section 44.
1980 c. 43.	The Magistrates' Courts Act 1980.	In section 142, in subsection (2), the words ", subject to subsection (4) below," and subsection (4).
1980 c. 47.	The Criminal Appeal (Northern Ireland) Act 1980.	Section 14. In section 16(1), the words "appeal or". In section 25(3), the words following "compellable". In section 44(4), the words "14 or".
1981 c. 54.	The Supreme Court Act 1981.	In Schedule 5, the entries relating to the Army Act 1955 and the Air Force Act 1955.
S.I. 1986/595 (N.I. 4).	The Mental Health (Northern Ireland) Order 1986.	In Schedule 5, in Part I, the entry relating to section 14(1) of the Criminal Appeal (Northern Ireland) Act 1980.
1988 c. 33.	The Criminal Justice Act 1988.	In section 133(5)(b), sub-paragraph (iii) and the word "or" immediately preceding it.
1991 c. 25.	The Criminal Procedure (Insanity and Unfitness to Plead) Act 1991.	In Schedule 3, paragraphs 3(1) and 4.